Vorwort

Mit dem hier vorgelegten Band "Old World Killis II" komplementieren wir die Killifische der Alten Welt. Waren im ersten Band mit den eigentlich nicht mehr zu den Killifischen gezählten Oryzias-Arten und ihren Verwandten sowie den Leuchtaugenfischen und der Gattung Aphyosemion im wesentlichen drei Großgruppen vertreten, von denen allein die Aphyosemion-Arten mehr als die Hälfte des Buches ausmachten, so enthält dieser Band II alle übrigen Killifische Asiens, Afrikas und Europas.

Den Schwerpunkt bilden dabei die Hechtlinge und die Nothobranchius-Arten, die aufgrund ihrer Farbigkeit und nicht zuletzt wegen ihrer leichten Züchtbarkeit in der Aquaristik beliebte Pfleglinge sind. Überdies ist die Ökologie der Nothobranchius-Arten als Saisonfische hochinteressant, und hierzu haben sie uns noch lange nicht alle ihre Geheimnisse offenbart. So lassen sich die Eier vieler Arten in Gefangenschaft - bei relativ hohen Temperaturen von 28-30° C gelagert - schon nach rund 6-8 Wochen aufgießen, sie sind dann also schlupfreif. In der Natur müssen die Eier bei nicht selten wesentlich höheren Temperaturen eine deutlich längere Zeit im Boden verbringen, der in der Trockenzeit zumeist betonhart ist. Diese Widersprüche und bemerkenswerten ökologischen Gegebenheiten sind im natürlichen Lebensraum bisher nahezu nicht untersucht worden. Gleich mehrere der in diesem Band II vorgestellten Gattungen sind ebenfalls Saisonfische und unterliegen ähnlichen Lebensbedingungen wie die Nothobranchius-Arten.

Einen gewissen Schwerpunkt dieses Bandes bilden auch die Aphanius-Arten der Alten Welt. Sie kommen gleich auf allen drei Kontinenten Europa, Asien und Afrika vor. Vermutlich sind sie zusammen mit der rein europäischen Gattung Valencia auch die am stärksten gefährdete Gruppe von Killifischen. In Spanien etwa sind die Lebensräume der beiden Arten Aphanius iberus und Valencia hispanica nachweislich drastisch zurückgegangen. Auch der Tourist kann an den Küsten Spaniens feststellen, daß so mancher Fluß heute nicht mehr das Meer erreicht, denn er wird schon zuvor für Bewässerungszwecke genutzt; Feuchtbereiche in Küstennähe, der Vorzugslebensraum beider Arten, werden trockengelegt und zugeschüttet, nicht selten mit "wilden" Müllkippen. Den Rest besorgen möglicherweise ausgesetzte Fische, die mit den einheimischen Arten konkurrieren, etwa Gambusia- oder neuerdings sogar Fundulus-Arten der Neuen Welt. Ähnliche Vorkommnisse scheinen in Nordafrika und der Türkei sowie dem Vorderen Orient nicht nur die Ausnahme zu sein. In der Azraq Oase, Jordanien, ist der nur hier vorkommende Aphanius sirhani stark gefährdet. Schutzmaßnahmen sind für mehrere Aphanius- und die Valencia-Arten also dringend erforderlich.

Wir haben in diesem Buch relativ viele Aphanius-Populationen zum Beispiel aus Spanien abbilden können. Hoffen wir, daß diese Dokumentation nicht etwa Erinnerungswert gewinnen wird, indem sie die Formen zeigt, die in wenigen Jahren verschwunden sein werden, hoffen wir vielmehr, daß sie Grundlagen für den Schutz und Erhalt dieser Populationen und ihrer Lebensräume bieten möge.

Foreword

This second volume o. AQUALOG's series on t concentrates on three i are, seen strictly scientii half of the book's space, ..hyosemion, OLD WORLD KILLIS II presents all other killis from Asia, Africa, and Europe.

The book mainly focuses on Panchaxes and Nothobranchius species, both being highly popular among hobbyists because of their bright colours and the easiness of breeding them in the aquarium. Moreover, the ecology of Nothobranchs as seasonal fishes is an immensely interesting field of study with many secrets that are still well kept. For example, in captivity eggs of many species are ready for hatching after having been kept at very high temperatures (28-30°C) for 6-8 weeks. In nature, the eggs have to stay a much longer period in the sometimes concrete-like soil, at very often considerably higher temperatures. These contradictions and the remarkable ecological circumstances under which these fishes exist have never been examined in the natural habitats. Several genera introduced in this book are also seasonal fishes and live under similar circumstances as Nothobranchs.

Another main emphasis is put on Aphanius species. This genus is endemic to all three continents of the Old World, Africa, Asia, and Europe. Together with the purely European genus Valencia, these species are probably the most endangered group of killifishes. In Spain, for example, the habitats of both species, Aphanius iberus and Valencia hispanica, have alarmingly decreased. Even tourists will recognise that, at the coastal line, many rivers vanish before they reach the sea because their water is used for agricultural purposes. The preferred habitats of the species, marshlands near the coast, are drained or filled up and, quite often, used as garbage dumps. And finally, released, foreign species like Gambusia or even Fundulus species from the New World compete with the endemic fish and, often enough, drive them out. The same thing seems to take place in North Africa and Turkey, also in the Near and Middle East. Here, Aphanius sirhani, a species that occurs exclusively in the Azraq Oasis (Jordan) is very much in danger of dying out. Several Aphanius and Valencia species are desperately in need of being put under protection.

In this book, we were able to show many Aphanius populations from, for example, Spain. Let's hope that these pictures will not become a memorial for the great variety of these beautiful fishes but the basis of our endeavours to save and protect both, fishes and habitats.

Mörfelden-Walldorf, August 1997

Publishers and author

Die Saisonfische der Alten Welt und ihre besonderen Anpassungen an die Lebensräume

Die Killifische der Alten Welt kommen in einer Vielzahl unterschiedlicher Lebensräume vor. Sie sind an diese zum Teil extremen Biotope in ganz hervorragender Weise angepaßt. Besonders manche Aplocheilidae haben Lebensräume erobert, in die ihnen andere Fische nicht folgen können, so etwa saisonale Gewässer, die periodisch austrocknen. Um derartige im Grunde lebensfeindliche Bereiche nutzen zu können, mußten ganz besondere Überlebensstrategien entwickelt werden.

Die meisten Killifische der Alten Welt kommen im Bereich des tropischen Regenwaldes und angrenzender Gebiete West- und Zentralafrikas vor. Die Tiere sind in der Regel klein und laufen daher Gefahr, leicht eine Beute von Feinden zu werden, zumal sie zumindest über größere Strecken auch keine sehr guten Schwimmer sind, wie der Vergleich einer *Aphyosemion*-Art mit einem Salmler oder einer Barbe rasch verdeutlicht. Die einfachste Möglichkeit, diesem Konkurrenzdruck auszuweichen, besteht darin, solche Lebensräume zu besiedeln, in die größere Fische, also eventuelle Raubfeinde, nicht oder nicht so leicht gelangen können. So finden sich viele Killifische der tropischen Regenwaldbereiche vorzugsweise am Rande der Gewässer im unmittelbaren Uferbereich. Hier wächst auch häufig eine Unterwasserflora oder Pflanzen des Landes ragen ins Wasser, wie etwa Sträucher und Gräser. Zwischen diesen lebenden Pflanzen und zum Teil abgestorbenen Ästen finden die kleineren Killifische Deckung. Oft sind solche Lebensräume auch außerordentlich flach, manche Arten bevorzugen überhaupt nicht das offene Wasser, sie sind vielmehr zwischen Laubblättern der Landbäume zu finden, die kleine Restpfützen oder Feuchtbereiche anfüllen. Um solche Lebensräume zu erreichen oder bei zu starker Austrocknung verlassen zu können, vermögen manche Killifische erstaunlich gut und gezielt zu springen. "Weltmeister" sind in dieser Hinsicht zwar die *Rivulus*-Arten der Neuen Welt, unter den Altweltkillifischen stehen ihnen manche *Aphyosemion*-Arten aber nicht so sehr stark nach. Auch die Hechtlinge vermögen ganz ordentlich zu springen. Für die Pflege dieser Arten bedeutet dies, daß eine dicht schließende Abdeckscheibe für das Aquarium unerläßlich ist.

Die allermeisten Fische meiden auch Sumpfgebiete. Derartige Lebensräume sind vom Wechsel der Niederschläge sehr stark abhängig, und häufig besteht hier die Gefahr des Austrocknens. Für gute Schwimmer fehlt hier überdies häufig der notwendige offene Schwimmraum. Sumpfbereiche wären also ein idealer Lebensraum um dem Feinddruck zu entgehen, doch unterliegen natürlich auch jene Fische den schwankenden Wasserverhältnissen, die solche Biotope als Rückzugsgebiete gerne nutzen würden. Da haben sich zahlreiche Killifische etwas "einfallen" lassen. Die Evolution hat sie in diesem Problembereich zu Saisonfischen werden lassen. Aufgrund der Auslese durch die Umwelt sind sie eng an den Wechsel des Wasserstandes angepaßt worden, der ja meist durch die Abfolge von Regen- und Trockenzeit bedingt ist. Das feinere Einwirken der Mechanismen in dieses Wechselspiel ist noch nicht ganz verstanden, die gröberen Umstände kennen wir aber schon.

Die Grundvoraussetzung einer Anpassung an saisonale Lebensräume ist ein sehr rasches Wachstum und ein sehr schnelles Erreichen der Geschlechtsreife. Ferner ist es von erheblichem Vorteil, wenn die Geschlechtsprodukte nicht auf einmal abgesetzt werden, sondern wenn dies unregelmäßig über einen längeren Zeitraum hinweg erfolgt. Das verringert das Risiko, daß der gesamte Nachwuchs auf einmal vernichtet wird. Wenn z.B. ein Cichlidengelege von Offenbrütern durch Trockenfallen vernichtet wird, dann sind - sagen wir - 500 Eier oder Jungfische vernichtet, wären diese Eier über einen längeren Zeitraum hinweg abgegeben worden, so wäre die Chance größer, daß immer noch einige Eier zur Entwicklung gelangen und die Art überleben lassen. Cichliden bevorzugen eben andere Lebensbereiche, in denen solche Gefahren nicht auftreten.

Wenn unsere Killifische sich also in saisonale Lebensräume zurückziehen um dem Feinddruck entgehen zu können, dann muß überdies gesichert sein, daß sie dann ihre volle Lebenskraft entfalten können, wenn auch der Wasserstand am höchsten ist, optimaler Wasserstand oder überhaupt vorhandenes Wasser und Fortpflanzungsperiode müssen also übereinstimmen. Dies bedeutet andererseits, daß zu Zeiten von Niedrigwasser oder fehlendem Wasser die Lebensfunktionen eingeschränkt sein müssen. Große Fische, die ebenfalls solche Lebensräume besiedeln, fallen dann in eine Trockenstarre, etwa die Lungenfische. Bei unseren kleinen Killifischen ist es das Eistadium, das diese ungünstige Zeit überdauert, während die erwachsenen Fische nur eine Feuchtigkeitsperiode erleben. Saisonfische gibt es im Bereich des Tropenwaldes, vor allem aber in der Savanne. Als die typischen Saisonfische schlechthin unter den Killis der Alten Welt gelten die *Nothobranchius*-Arten. Bei Ihnen ist die Anpassung an den Wechsel von Regen- und Trockenzeiten außerordentlich gut entwickelt. Die Elterntiere sind Dauerlaicher und Bodenlaicher. Sobald sie geschlechtsreif geworden sind, balzen die bunten Männchen die meist einfarbig graubraunen Weibchen an (siehe Tafel Seite 72). Es sind die Weibchen, die entscheiden, ob und mit welchem Partner sie ablaichen. Dies ist vor allem dann wichtig, wenn mehr als eine *Nothobranchius*-Art in einem Gewässer vorkommen, und das ist zumindest im Küsteneinzug Tanzanias eher die Regel als die Ausnahme. Ganz sicher ist der Selektionsdruck auf die Männchen, ein buntes Farbkleid zu entwickeln, von den Weibchen ausgegangen. Ist ein Weibchen laichbereit, dann schwimmt es zum Bodengrund hin, wobei ihm das Männchen folgt, mit dem Unterkopf in ständigem Kontakt zum Oberkopf und Nacken des Weibchens. Es sieht aus, als dirigiere das Männchen seine Partnerin zum Bodengrund. Ist das Weibchen nicht laichbereit, so flieht es vor dem Männchen, oft wird es von diesem dabei auch verfolgt und attackiert. In zu kleinen Aquarien kann dies, wenn das Weibchen nicht laichbereit ist, zum Tode des Tieres führen, in der Natur wird sich das Weibchen stets problemlos dem verfolgenden Männchen entziehen können. Bei einem ablaichbereiten Weibchen umgreift das Männchen mit seiner Rücken- und Afterflosse den Hinterleib der Partnerin und beide drücken sich fest gegen oder sogar in den Bodengrund. Das *Nothobranchius*-Weibchen hat mit seiner Afterflosse eine spitze Tüte gefaltet, mit der nun ein Ei in den Bodengrund gedrückt wird. Durch das Umgreifen des Weibchens durch das Männchen wird erzielt, daß die Befruchtungswahr-

Killifishes of the World
Old World Killis II

Dr. Lothar Seegers

Verlag: A.C.S. GmbH, Germany

Inhalt
Contents

Erklärungen der Abkürzungen in den wissenschaftlichen Namen
Key to the abbreviations of the scientific names

Beispiel/ *example:*	*Epiplatys* Gattung *Genus*	*dageti* Art *Species*	*monroviae* Unterart *Subspecies*	DAGET & ARNOULT, Beschreiber *Describer*	1964 Publikationsjahr *Year of publication*

sp./spec.: = species (lat.): Art/*species*
Hinter einem Gattungsnamen meint dies: Ein Artname steht (noch) nicht zur Verfügung, die Art ist bislang nicht eindeutig bestimmt bzw. noch nicht formell beschrieben./
Following the genus name, this means: A species name is not yet available, the species has not yet been determined or formally described.

ssp.: = subspecies (lat.): Unterart/*subspecies*
Einige Arten haben ein sehr großes Verbreitungsgebiet; innerhalb dieses Gebietes gibt es Populationen, die sich äußerlich zwar deutlich von anderen Populationen unterscheiden, genetisch jedoch zur gleichen Art gehören. Solche Populationen erhalten als Unterart einen wissenschaftlichen Namen. Ist die Unterart bislang unbenannt, so steht hier nur ssp./
Some species inhabit an area of a very wide range; within this area, there may be populations which differ significantly in appearance from other populations, but clearly belong to the same species. Such populations may get a third scientific name, indicating a subspecies. If a subspecies name has not yet been formally given, the abbreviation ssp. is added.

cf.: = confer (lat.): vergleiche/*compare*
Einem Artnamen vorangestellt meint dies: Das vorliegende Exemplar oder die entsprechende Population weicht in gewissen Details von der typischen Form ab, jedoch nicht so gravierend, daß es oder sie einer anderen Art zugeordnet werden könnte./
Placed in front of a species name this means: The specimen shown or the respective population to which it belongs differ in some minor details from the typical form, but these differences do not justify to place it into a species of its own.

sp. aff.: = species affinis (lat.): ... ähnliche Art/*similar to ...*
Einem Artnamen vorangestellt meint dies: Die vorliegende Art ist bisher noch nicht bestimmt, sie ähnelt jedoch der genannten und bereits beschriebenen Art./
Placed in front of a species name, this means: The species at hand is not yet determined but it is very similar to the one named in the following.

Hybride/*hybrid*: Kreuzungsprodukt, Mischling zweier Arten/*hybrid or crossbreed of two species*

scheinlichkeit des Eies durch die abgegebenen Spermien erhöht wird. Mit einem Ruck trennt sich das Paar voneinander, wodurch das Ei noch tiefer in den Bodengrund geschleudert wird.

Solange ein Saisonfisch lebt, wird ständig abgelaicht, es müssen viele Hunderte von Eiern sein, die auf diese Weise in den Bodengrund gelangen. Die Elterntiere sterben spätestens mit dem Austrocknen des Heimatgewässers, aber die Eier entwickeln sich langsam in dem in der Trockenzeit oft zementharten ehemaligen Gewässerboden. Dabei werden Entwicklungsstillstände eingelegt, sogenannte Dia-

pausen, um das Ei genau dann schlupfreif werden zu lassen, wenn die kommende Regenzeit einsetzt. Untersuchungen haben gezeigt (PETERS, 1963), daß die schlupfreifen Larven die Eihülle sprengen, wenn nach dem Einsetzen des Regens durch die sich nun ebenfalls entwickelnden Infusorien ein Sauerstoffmangel auftritt. In der Tat kann der Aquarianer schlupfreife Larven zum Verlassen der Eihülle bringen, indem er Trockenfutter auf die Wasseroberfläche streut. Alle Zusammenhänge dieses Systems sind allerdings noch nicht geklärt, denn in der Zucht entwickeln sich die Eier wesentlich rascher (8 Wochen) als

in der Natur, das Warum ist immer noch ein Geheimnis.

Viele Hunderte Eier und auch Jungfische sterben in der Natur während der Trockenzeit und bei einem erneuten, vorübergehenden, Austrocknen des Gewässers am Beginn der Regenzeit, es bleiben aber immer genügend lebensfähige Nachkommen übrig. Die Jungfische sind mit dem Schlüpfen schon relativ selbständig und gehen sogleich auf Futtersuche um schnell zu wachsen, ihrerseits die Geschlechtsreife zu erlangen und die Art zu erhalten.

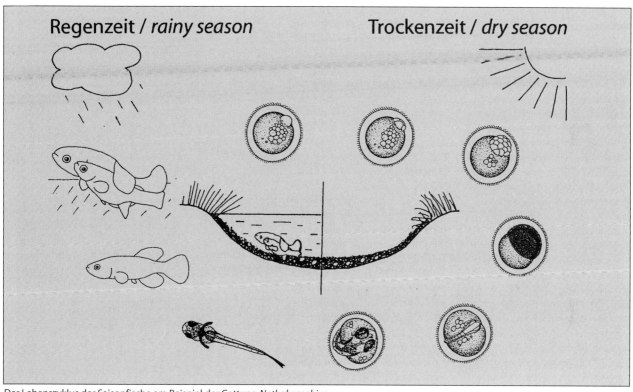

Der Lebenszyklus der Saisonfische am Beispiel der Gattung *Nothobranchius*.
The life cycle of seasonal fishes as, for example, in the genus Nothobranchius.

The seasonal killifishes of the Old World and their special adaptations to the environment

The killifishes of the Old World occur in the most different habitats and have very well adapted to the sometimes extreme conditions under which they have to live. Especially some Aplocheilidae have made themselves their home in places where other fishes cannot follow, like seasonal bodies of water that dry up periodically. In order to survive in habitats where there is actually an abundance of any other fish species, they had to develop special strategies of survival.

Most killis from the Old World occur in the tropical regions of the western and central parts of the African rainforest and surrounding territories. Killifishes are usually small and slow-moving swimmers (as you can see if you compare, for example, a specimen of Aphyosemion to a tetra or a barb) and are therefore always in danger of being eaten by other, bigger fish. The easiest way of evading such threats is, of course, to get out of the way of the predators and populate places where other, bigger fish cannot or hardly get to. This is why many killifishes of the tropical rainforests can be found, most of the time, at the waters' edge, close to the banks.

Here, submerged plants grow and often grass or branches of shrubs growing on the banks hang into the water and provide safety and cover for the smaller species.

As most killis don't like to swim in the open water, they usually stay in shallow waters, some even prefer small pools filled with decaying leaves. To be able to reach these places or, when drying up, to leave them, some killis developed an amazing ability to jump. "Long Jump World Champions" are Rivulus from the New World, but some Aphyosemion from the Old World are not bad, either. Panchaxes are pretty good jumpers, too;

translated to aquarium keeping, this means that tanks with these fishes always have to be tightly covered.

Generally, fish don't like marshlands because such habitats are subject to weather changes, especially the amount of rain that falls; usually, there is the danger of the marshes eventually drying up. Also, in marshlands there is not enough free space for good swimmers. So, all things considered, marshy habitats would be the perfect place for small species that need to evade enemies - if they could only survive the deadly lack of water that is surely to come about.

Many killifishes managed to do just that; evolution equipped the small animals with abilities which guarantee their survival even under worst conditions: they became so-called seasonal fishes. Their behaviour and way of living is tightly connected and adapted to the changing seasons and the accompanying rains, e.g. the sequence of wet and dry season. The finer mechanisms are not yet known but roughly we can explain which behavioural oddities derived from these environmental peculiarities. The most fundamental requirement for adapting to seasonal habitats is fast growth and as fast reaching of sexual maturity. Also, it is important that the sexual products are not expelled in one single spawn but irregularly and over a longer period. This way, the risk of all eggs dying at once is diminished considerably. If, for example, the spawn of an open brooding cichlid would die because of dryness, about 500 eggs or young fish would be dead in one single stroke - a catastrophe that would not have happened if the eggs had been laid over a longer time span. The chances for the species' survival would be much higher because there'd still be some eggs left that could hatch. But - cichlids simply live in habitats where such dangers do not occur and accordingly, there is no need for them to spawn daily times in one mating season.

Recollecting the fact that killifishes live in such 'dangerous' places in order to get rid of their enemies, one immediately sees the need for them to grow as quickly as possible and reach full life force once the circumstances are favourable, that is, the water levels high. Put another way: water and mating season have to be present at the same time. This means also, that during the dry season or lack of water all life functions have to be reduced to the lowest possible level. Bigger fish living under such circumstances, like lungfish, fall into a diapause. In killis, the eggs have to bridge this period, while the adult fish only live as long as wet season lasts.

Seasonal fishes occur in the tropical rainforest but also, in fact mainly, in the savanna. Among the seasonal killis from the Old World, the Nothobranchs are regarded as the most 'typical'. In these fishes, the adaptation to the changes of the seasons is extremely well developed. The parents are permanent spawners and bottom brooders. As soon as they are sexually mature, the colourful males start courtshipping the mostly greyish-brown females (see table on p. 72). The females decide if and with which male they want to mate. This is especially important in waters where more than one Nothobranchius species occurs, like in most habitats of Tanzania's coastal areas. In all probability the males' fantastic colouring came about as a result of the females' selectiveness. Once a female is ready to spawn, it starts to swim towards the bottom, followed by the male that stays in permanent contact with her head and neck. This procedure looks as if the male 'conducts' the female towards the spot where the mating will take place. If the female is not ready to spawn, she tries to escape the male. Very often, the male literally hunts and attacks her which, in smaller aquaria, can lead to heavy injuries or even the death of the female, a tragedy never occurring in the wild because there, the female has enough space to elude without problems. In spawning pairs, the male holds the female's back part with his dorsal and anal fin and both animals press their bodies tightly to or even into the ground. The Nothobranchius female folds her anal fin like nozzle and forces the fertilised egg through this 'construction' into the ground. The fact that the male bends around the female's back part increases the chances of the egg's fertilization by the male's sperms. With a jerky movement the pair separates, forcing the egg even deeper into the substrate. A seasonal fish spawns constantly as long as it lives and hundreds of eggs are deposited in the ground by a pair during its lifetime. The parents die as soon as the habitat dries up but the eggs slowly develop in the dry, hot, sometimes cement-like soil. During this period, the development sometimes slows down to phases of dormancy, the so-called diapause, which allow the eggs to be ready to hatch as soon as the rainy season begins. Research (PETERS, 1963) has proved that the larvae actually hatch when after the rains have started the now also developing infusoria cause an oxygen-deficiency. In the aquarium hatching can be provoked by sprinkling some flake food on the water surface. But - the whole reproduction system holds some secrets which still have to be explained, like the fact that in captivity, the eggs develop much faster (about 8 weeks) than in nature.

Hundreds of eggs and young fish die during the dry season and at the beginning of the rainy season (when the habitats temporarily dry up again) but there are still enough survivors to guarantee the perpetuation of the species. After hatching, the young are relatively independent and immediately start to look for food. They grow up fast, become sexually mature and spawn, producing the next generation of seasonal killifishes.

 © Verlag A.C.S. GmbH

Die Gattungen
The genera

Aplocheilus

Die asiatischen Aplocheilidae werden nur durch die eine Gattung *Aplocheilus* repräsentiert, zugleich Typusgattung der Familie. Diese Gattung ist sehr weit verbreitet, sie umfaßt den gesamten südasiatischen Raum südlich des Himalaya, von Ostpakistan über Vorderindien bis Hinterindien sowie die Insulinde. Zwar ist der Gattungstypus *Aplocheilus panchax* relativ variabel gefärbt, dennoch aber ist es eigentlich erstaunlich, daß sich die Gattung innerhalb des riesigen Verbreitungsgebietes, das zu weiten Teilen auch nur von dieser Art bewohnt wird, relativ wenig aufgespalten hat. In ganz Asien gibt es nur 5 Arten, während die afrikanischen Hechtlinge, die mit *Aplocheilus* nahe verwandt sind, zahlreiche Arten umfassen. SCHEEL (1968, 1990) sah die Verwandtschaft zwischen beiden Gruppen sogar so eng, daß er nur eine einzige Gattung *Aplocheilus* anerkennen wollte, in die auch die afrikanischen Arten zu stellen seien. Allerdings ist ihm in diesem Punkt allgemein kaum gefolgt worden und die afrikanischen Hechtlinge werden auch hier als selbständige Gattung *Epiplatys* gesehen.

Wie oben angeführt, ist *A. panchax* die am weitesten verbreitete *Aplocheilus*-Art, mit Ausnahme der Südspitze des vorderindischen Kontinents markiert sie die Verbreitungsgrenzen der gesamten Gattung. Schon seit diese Art als Aquarienfisch importiert wurde, versuchte man die unterschiedliche Färbung der Tiere eigenständigen Unterarten zuzuordnen (KÖHLER, 1906, 1907; KLAUSEWITZ, 1957; MEINKEN, 1964), doch mehrfach wurde dem entgegengehalten, daß in manchen Populationen eine fast so große Variabilität auftritt, wie sie die gesamte Art umfaßt, und daß Unterarten deshalb nicht abzugrenzen sind (ARNOLD, 1906, 1907, 1911). Leider scheint die alte Diskussion gelegentlich wieder aufzuflammen, obgleich bisher kaum neue Argumente herangezogen wurden. Hier werden keine Unterarten von *A. panchax* aufgeführt.

In ähnlicher Weise wurde versucht, die "kleinen vorderindischen Hechtlinge" aufzuspalten und drei Arten zuzuordnen: *Aplocheilus blockii* (ARNOLD, 1911), *Aplocheilus parvus* (RAJ, 1916) und *Aplocheilus kirchmayeri* BERKENKAMP & ETZEL, 1986. Wildfänge nomineller *A. kirchmayeri* (Verbreitungsgebiet nach BERKENKAMP & ETZEL, 1986 Goa, Südwest-Indien) sind von Wildfängen aus Sri Lanka jedoch nicht zu unterscheiden, die nach BERKENKAMP & ETZEL (1986) *A. parvus* sein sollten (siehe Fotos S. 18/19). Auf Sri Lanka gibt es nach den vorliegenden Informationen jedenfalls zwei "kleine" Formen. Es scheint so zu sein, daß es insgesamt zwei "kleine vorderindische Hechtlinge" gibt, die beide sowohl auf Sri Lanka als auch auf dem Festland vorkommen: *A. blockii* (*A. kirchmayeri* einschließend) und *A. parvus*, letzterem ist das auf Sri Lanka gesammelte Tier auf Abb. S. 18 oben rechts zuzuordnen. *Aplocheilus kirchmayeri* wird hier deshalb als Synonym zu *A. blockii* angesehen, die Identität von *A. parvus* hierzu ist noch nicht ausreichend geklärt.

Aquaristisch sind alle Hechtlinge der Gattung *Aplocheilus* sehr zu empfehlen, auch für das sogenannte Gesellschaftsbecken, in dem verschiedene Arten gemeinsam gepflegt werden. Besonders bei den großen Arten ist jedoch zu bedenken, daß sie nicht mit zu kleinen Fischen vergesellschaftet werden dürfen, denn sie sind Räuber. Als oberflächenorientierte Fische springen sie überdies gerne.

Diapteron

Die Gattung *Diapteron* umfaßt nur 5 Arten, die alle eine recht geringe Körpergröße aufweisen und aufgrund ihrer schönen Färbung bei den Killifischfreunden sehr beliebt sind. Die Gattung scheint auf den Ivindo-Einzug in Gabun konzentriert zu sein, wobei neuere Aufsammlungen auch Funde im unteren Ogowe-Einzug erbrachten, in den der Ivindo mündet.

Die Fische, die hier in eine eigenständige Gattung *Diapteron*

Aplocheilus

The Asian Aplocheilidae are represented by one single genus, Aplocheilus, which is also the type genus. The genus is widely distributed in Asia, from eastern Pakistan to the whole of South-West Asia south of the Himalayas, including the Indian Peninsula, and South-East Asia including the South-East Asian Islands. The almost omnipresent genus type, Aplocheilus panchax, is quite variable in colouration, but it is still amazing that - keeping the enormous distribution area in mind - the genus has split into such a relatively small number of species. In whole Asia, there are only 5 species whereas the African Panchaxes (close relatives) have numerous species. SCHEEL (1968, 1990) saw such a close relationship between the two genera that he proposed to unite the Asian and the African species under the collective genus name Aplocheilus. But he didn't have much approval in this regard, and this book, too, treats the African Panchaxes as a separate genus, Epiplatys. As I mentioned before, A. panchax is the most widely distributed Aplocheilus species and its occurrence marks (except the most southern parts of the Indian Peninsula) the boundaries of the whole genus's distribution area. Since the first imports of these fishes, it has been attempted to assign the variedly coloured strains to independent subspecies (KÖHLER, 1906, 1907; KLAUSEWITZ, 1957; MEINKEN, 1964). But as repeatedly as these attempts

Aplocheilus panchax

were made they were rejected because the colour variations within certain populations were as numerous as in the whole species and, accordingly, no definite subspecies could be identified (ARNOLD, 1906, 1907, 1911). Unfortunately, the discussion has not ceased although no new arguments are available; in this book, subspecies of A. panchax are not considered. Similarly, it was attempted to split up the "small South Asian Panchaxes" and assign them to three different species: Aplocheilus blockii (ARNOLD, 1911), Aplocheilus parvus (RAJ, 1916) and Aplocheilus kirchmayeri BERKENKAMP & ETZEL, 1986. Wildcaughts of acclaimed A. kirchmayeri (distribution area according to BERKENKAMP & ETZEL, 1986 Goa and South-West India) cannot be distinguished from wildcaughts from Sri Lanka that were identified by BERKENKAMP & ETZEL as A. parvus (see photos p.18/19). At the moment, available information imply that two 'small' forms occur in Sri Lanka. It seems as though there are altogether two "small South Asian Panchaxes", being endemic to both, Sri Lanka and the mainland: A. blockii (including A. kirchmayeri) and A. parvus (the latter being the correct identification of the fish shown in the photo on page 18, top right). A. kirchmayeri is regarded as a synonym of A. blockii, A. parvus is still not securely identified. For the hobby, all Panchaxes of the genus Aplocheilus can be warmly recommended, also for so-called community tanks. In the larger species one has to remember not to accompany them with smaller fishes because Panchaxes are predators. Like many other killifishes, they live surface-oriented and like to jump, so keep your tank tightly covered.

Diapteron

The genus Diapteron has five species all of which are relatively small but are highly popular among hobbyists because of their

gestellt werden, finden sich in der Liebhaber-Literatur auch in der Gattung *Aphyosemion*. Es erscheint deshalb sinnvoll, hier auf dieses Problem einzugehen. *Diapteron* wurde ursprünglich als Untergattung zu *Aphyosemion* beschrieben (HUBER & SEEGERS, 1977), von SEEGERS (1980) dann zur Gattung erhoben. PARENTI (1981) listet *Diapteron* wertfrei als Untergattung auf, denn sie konnte die Arbeit von SEEGERS (1980) noch nicht berücksichtigen, ferner untersuchte sie kein Material der Gattung. LAZARA (1987) bestätigt dies, bevorzugt jedoch die Einordnung von *Diapteron* als Untergattung. Gründe dafür werden nicht recht deutlich, zumal der Autor selbst feststellt: "Die *Diapteron*-Gruppe ist so auffällig, daß jeder das Bedürfnis verspüren muß, sie als einzigartig, als ganz speziell anzusehen.". Er bestätigt ferner, daß der Gattungsname den Nomenklaturregeln entsprechend vergeben wurde, schreibt überdies, die Gattung "ist wahrscheinlich monophyletisch, das heißt, die Mitglieder von *Diapteron* sind untereinander enger verwandt als mit irgendeiner Art oder Artengruppe außerhalb von *Diapteron*.". Nichts anderes wird durch eine Einordnung der betreffenden Arten in eine eigenständige Gattung *Diapteron* durch SEEGERS (1980) festgestellt: Es ist eine Gruppe von Arten als phylogenetisch zusammengehörig erkannt worden - dies sieht auch LAZARA so -, also ist diese Zusammengehörigkeit auch durch die entsprechende Benennung zu dokumentieren. Wenn LAZARA vorschlägt, "*Diapteron* sollte bis zu einer Revision (Überarbeitung) von *Aphyosemion* und verwandten Gattungen als Untergattung beibehalten werden.", so ist das ein Widerspruch in sich: Warum soll die Artengruppe als <u>Untergattung</u> beibehalten werden, nicht aber als Gattung? Entweder sie ist monophyletisch (wie auch LAZARA annimmt), dann ist es auch sinnvoll, sie als Gattung zu kennzeichnen, oder sie ist es nicht, dann wäre *Diapteron* auch als Untergattung hinfällig.

Merkwürdig ist ferner, daß *Fundulopanchax* als wesentlich schlechter definierte Artengruppe von *Aphyosemion* auf Gattungsebene getrennt werden soll, obgleich es neben anderen Gemeinsamkeiten beider nomineller Artengruppen zwischen verschiedenen Arten quer über die "Gattungs"-grenzen Kreuzungsprodukte gibt (siehe Band I dieser Reihe: SEEGERS, 1997, Seite 129). Kreuzungsprodukte zwischen *Diapteron*-Arten und verwandten Arten sind demgegenüber bisher nicht nachgewiesen worden, auch und besonders nicht solche mit *Aphyosemion*-Arten im engeren Sinne. Kreuzungen können sicher nicht die Entscheidung über eine Einordnung liefern, dies wird oft überschätzt, wohl aber liefern sie zusätzliche Hinweise. *Diapteron* ist also eine phylogenetisch sehr gut abgegrenzte monophyletische Artengruppe, die taxonomisch als eigenständige Gattung zu bezeichnen ist.

Aquaristisch sind die *Diapteron*-Arten kleine Kostbarkeiten, die erhebliche Aufmerksamkeit benötigen. Sie sind im Artenbecken zu pflegen, das nicht zu groß sein sollte, und das mit Torffasern und Javamoos eingerichtet werden kann. Nicht zu großes Lebendfutter ist wesentlich. Die Temperatur wird oft zu hoch eingestellt, 20 bis höchstens 24°C, eher der untere Bereich, sind völlig ausreichend.

Epiplatys

Die Hechtlinge Afrikas sind in einem großen Gebiet vom Sahelbereich im Norden (Senegambien im Westen bis mittlerer Nileinzug im Osten) bis zum südlichen Rand des westlichen Kongobeckens zu finden. Nach Osten überschreiten sie den Zentralafrikanischen Graben nicht. Auch der obere Zaïre beherbergt keine *Epiplatys*-Arten. Damit stellt sich die Gattung als vorwiegend west- und zentralafrikanisch dar. An den Urwald, der diesen Raum als dominierende Vegetationszone einnimmt, ist die Gattung aber nicht gebunden, denn es gibt typische Savannenarten wie *E. bifasciatus*, *E. spilargyreius* und andere.

Es wurde schon oben darauf hingewiesen, daß SCHEEL (1968, 1990) die afrikanische Gattung *Epiplatys* nicht anerkannte und sie als Synonym zur asiatischen Gattung *Aplocheilus* sah. Beide Gruppen sind sich in ihrer Gestalt und Lebensweise in

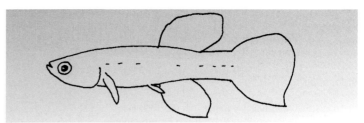

Diapteron georgiae

fantastic colours. The genus seems to occur mainly in the Ivindo-basin in Gabon, but lately also collections from the lower Ogowe-basin where the Ivindo joins the Ogowe have been reported. The fish that are assigned in this book to the independent genus Diapteron can sometimes be found in enthusiast literature as members of the genus Aphyosemion. I would like to discuss this problem a little bit. At first, Diapteron was classified as a subgenus of Aphyosemion (HUBER & SEEGERS, 1977), later it was raised to genus status (SEEGERS, 1980). PARENTI (1981) still listed Diapteron as a subgenus but she couldn't take SEEGERS´ paper into account and further didn't examine any material. LAZARA (1987) confirmed these details but nevertheless preferred in his own classification Diapteron as a subgenus. He also confirmed that the genus name had been assigned according to the nomenclature rules and that, in all probability, the species group is monophyletic, i.e. all members of the Diapteron group are more closely related to each other than to any other species or group of species outside Diapteron. This is exactly the same point SEEGERS made in his 1980 classification: He identified a phylogenetic species group (just like LAZARA did) and documented this fact by applying a separate name to this group of fishes. LAZARA contradicts himself in saying that Diapteron should be classified as a subgenus of Aphyosemion and related genera until a thorough revision has been carried out. But why should a clearly defined species group be classified as a subgenus and not as an independent genus? If a species group is monophyletic (like LAZARA admits) it is correct to classify it as a genus; if not, the classification of Diapteron as subgenus is invalid anyway. Further astonishment is aroused by taking a close look at the genus Fundulopanchax, a much less clearly defined species group than Diapteron that is still seen as a genus independent from Aphyosemion although (besides other shared characteristics) there are documented hybrids of Fundulopanchax and Aphyosemion (see: SEEGERS, Old World Killis I, p. 129). On the other hand, there are no reported crossbreeds of Diapteron and species of closely related species groups, especially not of Diapteron and Aphyosemion in the narrow sense. I am well aware that hybrids are not the main argument deciding whether a group of fishes can be classified as an independent genus but in this as in many other cases it can be a vital clue. Diapteron is a phylogenetically very well defined, monophyletic species group that has to be classified as a taxonomically independent genus.

In the hobby, all Diapteron species are precious little jewels that need a lot of attention and thoughtful care. They have to be tended in species tanks which should not be too large but well furnished with Java moss and peat. Rather small live food is essential. Water temperature is often too high, it should be between 20 and 24°C, the lower degree being absolutely sufficient.

Epiplatys

The African panchaxes are widely distributed from the Sahel regions in the north (Senegambia in the west to the middle basin of the river Nile in the east) to the southern borders of the western Congo basin. To the east, they do not spread out farther than the Great Rift Valley. Also, Epiplatys do not occur in

der Tat verblüffend ähnlich. So sind es Oberflächenfische und Räuber, beide haben mehr oder minder deutliche silberfarbene oder doch helle Schuppen auf der Oberseite des Kopfes. Sie lauern zwischen den Pflanzen oder anderer Deckung auf Beute, die zumeist aus Insekten besteht. Es werden aber durchaus auch kleine Fische gefressen. Hier wird die Gattung *Epiplatys* als eigenständig gesehen. Innerhalb des großen Verbreitungsgebietes gibt es gewisse Gattungsgruppen, von denen insbesondere drei herausragen: Die beiden westafrikanischen Gruppen um *Epiplatys dageti* und *E. fasciolatus*, sowie die *E. sexfasciatus*-Gruppe, die sich entlang des Küsteneinzuges von Ost-Ghana bis Gabun erstreckt. Eine vierte Gruppe ist besonders undurchsichtig, sie bewohnt das Kongobecken und seine nördlichen Rand-

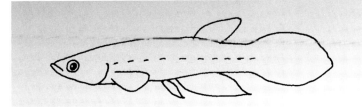

Epiplatys sexfasciatus

zonen, es ist die *E. chevalieri/E. multifasciatus*-Gruppe. Im Verlaufe mehrerer Sammelreisen fanden ETZEL und Mitreisende eine Reihe von Phänotypen einer *Epiplatys*-Artengruppe, die ihn und BERKENKAMP dazu anregten, eine Fülle neuer Arten und Unterarten zu beschreiben, wobei auch Material anderer Sammler mit einbezogen wurde, etwa von ROLOFF. Es sind dies - in alphabetischer Reihenfolge - die Arten *E. azureus* BERKENKAMP & ETZEL, 1983, *E. coccinatus* BERKENKAMP & ETZEL, 1982, *E. hildegardae* BERKENKAMP, 1983, *E. josianae* BERKENKAMP & ETZEL, 1983, *E. kassiapleuensis* BERKENKAMP & ETZEL, 1977, *E. fasciolatus puetzi* BERKENKAMP & ETZEL, 1986, *E. ruhkopfi* BERKENKAMP & ETZEL, 1980; *Epiplatys zimiensis* BERKENKAMP, 1977. Hinzu kommen *Epiplatys njalaensis* NEUMANN, 1976, *E. roloffi* ROMAND, 1978, *E. fasciolatus tototaensis* ROMAND, 1978 (Synonym: *Epiplatys fasciolatus huwaldi* BERKENKAMP & ETZEL, 1978), ferner *E. olbrechtsi dauresi* ROMAND, 1985 und *Epiplatys guineensis* ROMAND, 1994. Schon älteren Datums sind *Epiplatys fasciolatus* (GÜNTHER, 1866), *E. fasciolatus olbrechtsi* POLL, 1941 und auch *E. lamottei* DAGET, 1954. Dies sind insgesamt 16 mehr oder weniger nahe miteinander verwandte Arten oder Unterarten, eine außerordentliche Fülle, zu denen im gleichen Raum noch Hechtlinge anderer Arten oder gar Artengruppen hinzukommen. Heute erscheint - nicht zuletzt auch aufgrund der Tätigkeit von ETZEL - die Hechtlingsfauna Westafrikas als besser bekannt als in den 70er und 80er Jahren, und eine kritische Übersicht ist angebracht.
Zweifelsohne ist *E. fasciolatus* als zuerst beschriebene Art dieses Verwandtschaftskreises valide, "gute" Arten sind sicher auch *E. hildegardae*, *E. lamottei*, *E. njalaensis* und *E. roloffi*. *Epiplatys olbrechtsi* wurde als Unterart zu *E. fasciolatus* beschrieben, und dieser ursprünglichen Einordnung scheint die Zuordnung der Mehrheit der obengenannten Taxa am nächsten zu kommen. Fast alle oben genannten Taxa lassen sich problemlos in den *E. fasciolatus-olbrechtsi*-Formenkreis einordnen. Ob man diese oder jene Form als Unterart zu *E. fasciolatus* oder *E. olbrechtsi* sehen will, hängt von der Einschätzung des jeweiligen Betrachters ab, mir scheinen deutlich zuviele Taxa beschrieben worden zu sein. Exemplarisch wird das Problem am Beispiel des als *E. fasciolatus puetzi* beschriebenen, optisch sehr schönen Fisches, deutlich, der sicher *E. olbrechtsi* näher steht als *E. fasciolatus*. *Epiplatys olbrechtsi* sind augenscheinlich *azureus*, *kassiapleuensis*, *puetzi* und *dauresi* zuzuordnen, zu *E. fasciolatus* gehören *josianae*, *zimiensis* und *tototaensis*. Etwas aus der *E. olbrechtsi*-Gruppe heraus ragt *E. ruhkopfi*. *Epiplatys coccinatus* steht auch hier optisch zwischen dieser Art und *E. olbrechtsi*, doch könnten diese beiden Formen sich schon soweit von *E. olbrechtsi* entfernt haben, daß sie tatsächlich eine selbständige Art darstellen. Zu *E. guineensis* vermag ich gegenwärtig keine

upper Zaire or Congo, the genus being thus an almost exclusively West and Central African one. Still, the genus is not tied to the dominating jungle; there are many Epiplatys *species which are native to the savanna like* E. bifasciatus *and* E. spilargyreius. *It was mentioned above that* SCHEEL *(1968, 1990) did not accept* Epiplatys *as an independent genus but regarded it as a synonym of the Asian* Aplocheilus. *In fact, it is true that the two genera are very much alike in both behaviour and appearance. Both are surface fish and they are predators, both have more or less visible, silvery or at least light scales on their heads. They hide between plants or other hideouts waiting for prey, mostly insects, but sometimes also small live fish. In this book, the genus* Epiplatys *is accepted as independent.*
Within the wide distribution area of the genus, there are several groups which stand out from the rest: the Epiplatys dageti *group and* E. fasciolatus *group from West Africa and* E. sexfasciatus *group from the eastern coastal line reaching from East Ghana to Gabon. A fourth group is extremely obscure and occurs in the Congo basin and its northern margins: the* E. chevalieri/E. multifasciatus *group.*
In the course of several collecting trips, ETZEL *and his colleagues collected several phenotypes of an* Epiplatys *group which inspired him and* BERKENKAMP *to describe a whole lot of new species and subspecies taking into consideration also material collected by others, like* ROLOFF. *These new species are (in alphabetical order):* Epiplatys azureus BERKENKAMP & ETZEL, *1983,* E. coccinatus BERKENKAMP & ETZEL, *1982,* E. hildegardae BERKENKAMP, *1983,* E. josianae, BERKENKAMP & ETZEL, *1980,* E. kassiapleuensis BERKENKAMP & ETZEL, *1977,* E. fasciolatus puetzi BERKENKAMP & ETZEL, *1986,* E. ruhkopfi BERKENKAMP & ETZEL, *1980,* E. zimiensis BERKENKAMP, *1977. Further, there are* Epiplatys njalaensis NEUMANN, *1976,* E. roloffi ROMAND, *1978,* E. fasciolatus tototaensis ROMAND, *1978 (synonym of* Epiplatys fasciolatus huwaldi BERKENKAMP & ETZEL, *1978), as well as* E. olbrechtsi dauresi ROMAND, *1985 and* Epiplatys guineesis ROMAND, *1994. Some older species are* Epiplatys fasciolatus (GÜNTHER, *1866),* E. fasciolatus olbrechtsi POLL, *1941 and* E. lamottei DAGET, *1954. These are the 16 more or less closely related species and subspecies occurring in the same area, an area where several other species or species groups of panchaxes live. Today, not least thanks to the work of* ETZEL, *the panchax fauna of West Africa is much better known than 10 or 20 years ago; now a critical revision is reasonable.*
Being the first ever described species, E. fasciolatus *is without doubt a valid species of this group. Other "good" species are* E. hildegardae, E. lamottei, E. njalaensis *and* E. roloffi. Epiplatys olbrechtsi *was described as a subspecies of* E. fasciolatus, *and this original assignment seems to be useful for the classification of most taxa listed above. Almost all taxa can be assigned unproblematically to the* E. fasciolatus-olbrechti *group. Assigning the different subspecies to either* E. fasciolatus *or* E. olbrechti *depends largely on the observer's point of view, I think that way too many taxa have been described. Let me give one example:* E. fasciolatus puetzi *is a beautiful fish that is certainly closer related to* E. olbrechtsi *than to* E. fasciolatus. *Obviously,* E. azureus, kassiapleuensis, puetzi *and* dauresi *have to be assigned to the* Epiplatys olbrechtsi *group, whereas* E. josianae, zimiensis *and* tototaensis *belong to* Epiplatys fasciolatus. *A little bit outside the* E. olbrechtsi *group is* E. ruhkopfi. Epiplatys coccinatus *stands visually somehow between* E. olbrechtsi *and* E. ruhkopfi *but it resembles the latter so strongly, it seems possible that the two are so distant from* E. olbrechtsi *that they form an independent species indeed. At the moment, I cannot comment on* E. guineensis.
The Epiplatys sexfasciatus *group in the narrow sense inhabits the more or less coastal areas of the rainforest from Gabon to Togo/Ghana. The oldest available name was assigned by* GILL *in 1862, followed in 1866 by the name* E. infrafasciatus GÜNTHER *which has been regarded as a synonym of the first name ever*

Stellung zu nehmen.

Die *Epiplatys sexfasciatus*-Gruppe im engeren Sinne hat ihre Verbreitung in einem mehr oder weniger küstennahen Bereich vorwiegend des Regenwaldes von Gabun bis Togo/Ghana. Der älteste verfügbare Name wurde 1862 von GILL vergeben, dem 1866 der Name *infrafasciatus* GÜNTHER folgte, der bisher als Synonym zu ersterem betrachtet wurde. Seit den 70er Jahren wurden innerhalb des *E. sexfasciatus*-Kreises Unterarten ausgegliedert, denen, offensichtlich ohne die alten verfügbaren Namen ausreichend zu berücksichtigen, neue Namen gegeben wurden. Erst jüngst wurde der ältere Name *infrafasciatus* wieder in die Diskussion gebracht (STENGLEIN, 1993). Der Typenfundort für dieses Taxon ist "Old Calabar" in SO-Nigeria. In diesem Raum grenzen allerdings mindestens zwei der bisher als Unterarten angesehenen *E. sexfasciatus*-Populationen aneinander: Eine goldglänzende Form des Nigerdeltas, die möglicherweise der Unterart *E. s. togolensis* zuzuordnen ist (SCHEEL, 1990), und der bisher als *E. s. rathkei* bekannte Fisch. Es ist die Frage, welcher dieser beiden Formen die Typen von *infrafasciatus* zuzuordnen sind. STENGLEIN (1993) weist auf eine bisher nicht erschienene Arbeit WILDEKAMPS hin, in der die kamerunischen Formen alle zu *Epiplatys sexfasciatus infrafasciatus* gestellt werden, die Unterarten *rathkei* und *baroi* also synonymisiert werden. Eine Begründung dafür ist bisher wohl nicht publiziert worden. ETZEL (1996) unterscheidet drei Arten *E. sexfasciatus*, *E. infrafasciatus* und *E. togolensis*, wobei die bisherigen Unterarten *baroi* und *rathkei* zu *infrafasciatus* gestellt werden. Die Frage ist, welcher Population die Typen von *infrafasciatus* zugehören und ob zwischen den südkamerunischen und den gabunischen Hechtlingen dieses Formenkreises wirklich so deutliche Unterschiede bestehen. Solange die zu diesem Problem Stellung beziehenden Publikationen nicht erfolgt sind, wird hier der bisherige Gebrauch der Unterartnamen beibehalten, die Namenszuordnung mag sich aber tatsächlich in einiger Zeit berechtigterweise ändern.

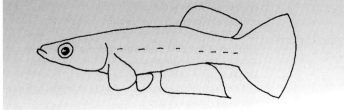

Episemion callipteron

Episemion

Episemion wird hier als Gattung aufgefaßt, obgleich sich seine Bearbeiter schon bei der Erstbeschreibung nicht so recht sicher waren, ob es sich um eine gültige Gattung oder um eine Untergattung zu *Epiplatys* handele. Es wird auf eine spätere Publikation zur Klärung der Einordnung verwiesen, die aber bisher nicht erschienen ist. Die bis heute bekannt gewordenen *Episemion*-Formen stehen vom Gesamthabitus her der Gattung *Aphyosemion* näher als der Gattung *Epiplatys*. Dabei ist keineswegs sicher, ob die Gattung *Episemion* nur die eine Art *callipteron* enthält, oder ob sie nicht mehrere Arten umfaßt. Die bisher importierten Tiere unterscheiden sich farblich, es mögen sich dahinter nur Farbformen einer Art oder aber auch mehrere Arten verbergen. *Episemion* sind stets kleine Raritäten, die keine weite Verbreitung erlangten und nur von wenigen Aquarianern gezüchtet wurden. In der Natur sollen diese Fische in sehr weichem und deutlich saurem Wasser vorkommen, auch im Aquarium sollte weiches Wasser mit einem sauren pH-Wert (pH 6) verwendet werden.

Foerschichthys

Die Einordnung der Fische, die der Gattung *Foerschichthys* zuzuordnen sind, hat geraume Zeit Kopfzerbrechen bereitet,

since. In the 70's, the *E. sexfasciatus group* was divided into several subspecies whose names were assigned obviously without considering the already existing ones. Only just recently, the old name *E. infrafasciatus has been reconsidered* (STENGLEIN, 1993). The type locality of this taxon is "Old Calabar" in SE-Nigeria. In this area, also two populations of *E. sexfasciatus occur that were in the past classified as subspecies: a golden form from the Niger delta that could belong to the subspecies E. s. togolensis* (SCHEEL, 1990), and the fish formerly known as E. s. rathkei. *Now it has to be decided to which of the two species the types of* infrafasciatus *have to be assigned to.* STENGLEIN (1993) *mentions an unknown paper of* WILDEKAMP *who suggests to place all forms from Cameroon in* Epiplatys sexfasciatus infrafasciatus, *that is, to synonymize the subspecies* E. rathkei *and* E. baroi. *The reasons for this suggestion have not been published.* ETZEL (1996) *distinguishes three species,* E. sexfasciatus, E. infrafasciatus, *and* E. togolensis, *assigning the two subspecies* rathkei *and* baroi *to* E. infrafasciatus. *It has to be decided to which of the two populations the type specimens of* infrafasciatus *belong to and whether the differences between the south Cameroonian and the Gabonian panchaxes are really significant. But as along as papers dealing with these problems have not been published, the names of the subspecies have to stay in use. Still, a justifiable change of this name order might come about in the near future.*

Episemion

Here, Episemion *is considered a separate genus although even the scientists who worked on its originaldescription didn't quite come to terms with the question whether* Episemion *is a separate genus or a subgenus of* Epiplatys. *In the first description, the authors refer to a final classification in a later publication which - unfortunately - has not been published until today. All forms of* Episemion *known at the moment are - in terms of behaviour - closer to* Aphyosemion *than to* Epiplatys. *Also, it is not quite clear whether this genus has only one single species (*Episemion callipteron*) or several.*

Specimens of Episemion *are always precious rarities which are not widely distributed in the hobby and which have been only scarcely bred by aquarists. In the wild, these fish are said to occur in very soft and clearly acidic water, accordingly they should be kept at home under similar conditions (pH 6).*

Foerschichthys

The classification of the fish assigned to the genus Foerschichthys *was a really difficult task although the genus has only one species. This species looks very much like a lampeye, and thus,* MEINKEN *called it in 1932* Aplocheilichthys flavipinnis. *In 1968,* SCHEEL *questioned the validity of* MEINKEN's *classification; he saw the fish more closely related to Rivulinae (today: Aplocheilidae), especially to* Aphyosemion. *He thought it justified to set up an independent genus, and some years later the genus* Foerschichthys SCHEEL & ROMAND, 1981 *was established. The non-annual* Foerschichthys flavipinnis *occur from the coastal drainages of SE Ghana to the Niger delta, living in schools in their habitats. In the aquarium, they are somewhat delicate pets that need live food meeting their size. Recommended accommodation is a small species tank.*

Fundulosoma

The genus Fundulosoma *is monotypical, too, it has only one, relatively small species.* Fundulosoma thierryi *is a typical seasonal fish, occurring in the savannas of Mali, Burkina Faso and from Nigeria to the coastal drainages of SE-Ghana and Togo. The classification of this fish that when first described was given not only a name but also independent genus status is also a point of discussion in the aquatic world.* SCHEEL (1968,

obgleich es sich nur um eine einzige Art handelt. Diese Art ähnelt sehr einem Leuchtaugenfisch, und so beschrieb MEINKEN (1932) die neue Art als *Aplocheilichthys flavipinnis*, als einen Aplocheilichthyiden also. SCHEEL (1968) bezweifelte die richtige Einordnung des Fisches durch MEINKEN, er sah eine nähere Verwandtschaft zu den Rivulinae (heute: Aplocheilidae), besonders zu *Aphyosemion*. Er hielt eine eigene Gattung für gerechtfertigt, und dieser Schritt wurde dann durch die Schaffung von *Foerschichthys* SCHEEL & ROMAND, 1981 vollzogen. Der nichtannuelle *Foerschichthys flavipinnis* findet sich im Küsteneinzug von Südost-Ghana bis zum Nigerdelta, die Tiere sollen in ihren Gewässern in Schulen zu finden sein.

Im Aquarium sind es etwas heikle Pfleglinge, die ihrer geringen Größe entsprechendes Lebendfutter benötigen. Am besten sind sie in einem kleineren Artenbecken untergebracht.

Fundulosoma

Auch die Gattung *Fundulosoma* ist monotypisch, auch sie umfaßt also nur eine einzige Art, die zudem ebenfalls relativ klein ist. *Fundulosoma thierryi* ist jedoch ein typischer Saisonfisch, der in den Savannen von Mali, Obervolta und Nigeria bis zum Küsteneinzug in Südost-Ghana und Togo vorkommt. Aber auch die Einordnung dieses schon bei seiner Beschreibung in eine eigene Gattung gestellten Fisches wird nicht einheitlich gesehen. SCHEEL (1968, 1990) diskutiert die Art und stellt fest, daß sie zwischen *Nothobranchius* und *Aphyosemion* stehe und daß eine eigene Gattung gerechtfertigt sei, PARENTI (1981) stellt die Art *thierryi* in die Gattung *Nothobranchius*. Bemerkenswert ist, daß gerade diese Art ovale Eier besitzt, während die Eier in der Gattung *Nothobranchius* im Gegensatz zur Gattungsdiagnose in PARENTI (1981: 480) in Wirklichkeit rund sind (SEEGERS, 1985).

In Gefangenschaft sollte dieser interessante Fisch im Artaquarium gepflegt werden. Als typischer Saisonfisch ist er wie ein Bodenlaicher zu züchten, wobei sich Torf als Ablaichmaterial bewährt hat. Die Art ist etwas empfindlich und benötigt regelmäßige Aufmerksamkeit.

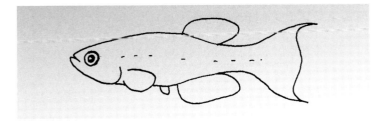

Fundulosoma thierryi

Nothobranchius

Die Gattung *Nothobranchius* ist die viertgrößte Gattung in der Familie Aplocheilidae und der erste aus Afrika beschriebene Aplocheilide ist *Nothobranchius orthonotus* (PETERS, 1844). *Nothobranchius*-Arten sind die typischen Saisonfische der Killifische der alten Welt, die Fische sind besonders an den Wechsel von Regen- und Trockenzeit in Steppe und Buschland angepaßt. Das Verbreitungsgebiet der Gattung reicht vom Tschad-Einzug und dem Sudan im Norden das Nilsystem aufwärts bis zum Viktoriasee und erstreckt sich ostwärts des zentralafrikanischen Grabenbruches nach Süden bis Natal in Südafrika. Ein Verbreitungsausläufer reicht den Sambesi aufwärts bis zum Chobe River und ferner den Kafue River entlang und dann, die Wasserscheide nordwärts überspringend, bis zum Luapula und den Upemba-Seen am Lualaba in der Zaïre-Provinz Shaba. Besonders in Tanzania findet sich dabei ein Schwerpunkt, nirgends gibt es soviele *Nothobranchius*-Arten wie hier (SEEGERS, 1985). Taxonomisch stellt sich die Gattung relativ problemlos dar, der Gattungsname *Nothobranchius* ist nie in Zweifel gezogen worden. Allerdings läßt sich die Gattung in Artengruppen aufgliedern.

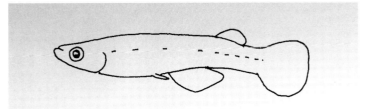

Foerschichthys flavipinnis

1990) discussed the species and resumed that it is placed between Nothobranchius and Aphyosemion *and therefore an independent genus is justified.* PARENTI (1981) *assigned the species* thierryi *to* Nothobranchius, *based on the false assumption that* Nothobranchius *species have oval eggs, which is indeed true in* Fundulosoma thierry, *but not in* Nothobranchius *- these fishes have round eggs* (PARENTI, 1981: 480). *In captivity, this interesting fish should be kept in a species tank. Being a typical seasonal fish, it breeds like a substratum-spawner and does fine in a tank with a peat covered bottom. The species is quite sensitive and needs attentive care.*

Nothobranchius

The genus Nothobranchius *is the forth largest genus of the family Aplocheilidae; the first ever described Aplocheilidae from Africa was* Nothobranchius orthonotus (PETERS, 1844). Nothobranchius *species are the most typical seasonal killis of the Old World, they have extremely well adapted to the changes of dry and rainy season in savanna and bush. The distribution area of the genus reaches from the Chad drainage to Sudan in the north along the Nile to Lake Victoria and east of the Great Rift Valley southwards to Natal in South Africa. One separate strain of distribution follows the river Sambesi upwards to the river Chobe and along the river Kafue and, passing the watershed to the north, continues in the Luapula and the Upemba-lakes at the river Lualaba in the province Shaba in Zaire.*

Especially in Tanzania, there is a definite Nothobranchius *centre, the majority of all known* Nothobranchius *species occur here* (SEEGERS, 1985). *Taxonomically, the genus is absolutely unproblematic, the genus name* Nothobranchius *was never doubted in any way, the genus, however, can be split up into species groups.*

MYERS (1924) *introduced* Adiniops *as a subgenus of* Aphyosemion, *type species is* Nothobranchius guntheri *as it is known today. In this species-group, there are a whole lot of close relatives all of which are relatively small and have a bright red caudal fin. These features hint toward their membership of the N. guentheri group, but these species cannot be classified as a subgenus of* Nothobranchius. Adiniops *is a simple synonym of* Nothobranchius.

Pronothobranchius *was originally suggested by* RADDA (1969) *as a subgenus of* Nothobranchius, *but in this book, this taxon is acknowledged as a valid genus. In the same article,* RADDA *proposed the subgenus* Zononothobranchius {not Zonothobranchius (PARENTI, 1981: 479)} *with the type* N. rubroreticulatus. *This subgenus is not valid, it is a simple synonym of* Nothobranchius.

Aphyobranchius WILDEKAMP, 1977 *with its two species* janpapi *and* luekei *could be accepted as a subgenus where other undescribed forms could also be assigned to; I don't feel like placing* N. willerti *in this group. The N. microlepis species group can also be seen as a separate unit, but it doesn't look as if it were closely related to* Paranothobranchius.

Nothobranchius orthonotus

MYERS (1924) stellte Adiniops als Untergattung zu Aphyosemion auf, Typus ist Nothobranchius guentheri im heutigen Sinne. Diese Art hat zwar eine ganze Reihe näherer Verwandter, die sich alle dadurch auszeichnen, daß sie relativ klein sind und eine intensiv rote Schwanzflosse aufweisen, so daß man von einer N. guentheri-Gruppe sprechen kann, doch lassen sich diese Arten nicht als Untergattung zu Nothobranchius einordnen. Adiniops ist ein simples Synonym zu Nothobranchius. Pronothobranchius wurde von RADDA (1969) ursprünglich als Untergattung zu Nothobranchius vorgeschlagen, hier wird das Taxon als eigene Gattung gesehen. In der gleichen Arbeit schlug RADDA eine Untergattung Zononothobranchius vor [nicht Zonothobranchius (PARENTI, 1981: 479)], mit der Typusart N. rubroreticulatus. Diese Untergattung kann nicht aufrecht erhalten werden, sie ist ein einfaches Synonym zu Nothobranchius. Aphyobranchius WILDEKAMP, 1977 läßt sich mit seinen beiden Arten janpapi und luekei durchaus als Untergattung begreifen, noch unbeschriebene Formen kommen hinzu, N. willerti vermag ich allerdings nicht hier einzuordnen. Auch die N. microlepis-Artengruppe läßt sich als Einheit sehen, sie hat aber mit Paranothobranchius wohl keine direkten näheren Verwandtschaftsbezüge.

Pachypanchax

Until a few years ago, there was little knowledge about this genus. Pachypanchax playfairii was for a very long time the only species present in the hobby, but at the same time, it is a hearty fish well suited for community tanks and therefore a steady inhabitant of aquaria for just as long. For a while, a fish from Madagascar called P. omalonotus could be found occasionally in the tanks of hobbyists. For several years now, forms of this genus have been more regularly imported from Madagascar, hinting at a certain variety. Still, it is unclear whether these fish can be assigned to the already described Madagascan species nuchisquamulatus and sakaramyi and if these species are valid or not; maybe further collections will show an even greater variety of Panchaxes from Madagascar. Until now, P. nuchisquamulatus was regarded as a synonym of P. omalonotus; as long as there is no further information on the issue, I follow this classification. The fish introduced in this book as P. sakaramyi was collected at the type locality from where the first specimens had been described. Whether the fish is a separate species indeed, or a colour variation of P. omalonotus, remains to be evaluated.

Pachypanchax playfairii

Description of Nothobranchius fuscotaeniatus *new species*

A peculiar Nothobranchius species from Tanzania is described here to introduce the name to the aquarium hobby because it can be expected that the new species will be available to interested aquarists within the next months.

Holotype: ZMB 32.781, male, 33.1 mm from snout to caudal origin (= standard length: SL) and 42.1 mm from snout to end of caudal fin (= total length: TL). Tanzania: Coast Region: Lower Rufiji drainage: about 2 km south of Ndundu Ferry across the Rufiji River on road from Nyamwage to Kibiti. L. SEEGERS, 22 July 1997.
Paratypes: ZMB 32.782, 3 males, 25.1-31.3 mm SL and 30.1-39.3 mm TL and ZMB 32.783, 6 females, 25.1-28.1 mm SL and 31.1-35.0 mm TL, collected with the holotype.
Diagnosis: This is the only known species of the genus in which the males are of an intense blue-green ground color with no red neither on the body nor in the fins and in which the females have a similar (although somewhat more subdued) color pattern than in males. No other Nothobranchius is known in which the females show distinct bars across the body. The color pattern is unique in the new species, see page 62.
Description (The variation of the measurements is given followed by the means in parenthesis and the data of the holotype in italics): As percent of SL: TL 119.9-130.7 (126.1) *127.2*; body depth: 26.6-32.3 (29.3) *30.5*; body width: 11.6-23.4 (14.8) *11.8*; head length: 32.4-36.3 (34.9) *35.6*; pectoral fin length: 16.3-21.5 (19.6) *21.5*; pelvic fin length: 8.0-12.3 (10.8) *9.7*; caudal peduncle length: 19.7-23.9 (21.8) *21.8*; caudal peduncle depth: 12.7-18.3 (15.4) *14.5*; predorsal length: 54.6-61.3 (58.7) *52.0*; prepelvic length: 42.8-52.6 (49.2) *50.2*; preanal length: 52.7-65.4 (60.9) *56.8*. As percent of head length: head width: 52.7-64.8 (58.9) *51.7*; snout length: 19.6-27.0 (23.8) *24.6*; eye diameter: 25.3-33.0 (30.2) *27.1*; interorbital distance: 40.7-48.3 (44.2) *40.7*; length of pectoral fin: 45.5-62.6 (56.1) *60.2*; length of pelvic fin: 22.5-34.5 (30.8) *27.1*.
Counts: dorsal fin rays: 8x15, 1x16, *16*; anal fin rays: 1x16, 8x17, *17*; scales in longitudinal line: 2x26, 6x27, 1x28 (26.9) *28*.
Seen from the side the form of the body is relatively deep and rhombic, the deepest part being between the dorsal and anal fin origins

which are in opposition to each other. The head is acute and the back is straight from the dorsal origin to the snout. Pelvics small, dorsal and anal relatively deep, especially the latter. The distal margin of the anal is straight and not convex as in most other species.
Life coloration: See page 62, center, showing the holotype, and page 62, bottom, showing two paratypes (male and female). In the male the ground color is of a bluish green, slightly lighter towards the belly. The back and upper head are brown. About 9-10 bars which are reddish-brown can be seen on the flanks, they may continue on the dorsal and proximal half of the anal fins. Both fins are edged white and have black submarginal bands in its hinder parts which are not sharply delimitated. The caudal fin is black in its posterior third, proximally a narrow yellow or greenish band is followed by a reddish band of about the same width. This again is followed proximally by a narrow bluegreen and a brown band, the caudal peduncle is green with some dark maculae.
Habitat and associated species: Collecting locality TZ 97/57 was a roadside ditch of about 2 m width and 10 m length which had a depth of up to about 60 cm. It was partly covered by high grass, especially near the margins, but there were some patches of open water. The fish were found mainly between the grass. Together with the new species many Nothobranchius janpapi WILDEKAMP, 1977 were collected (see photos of specimens from this locality on pages 64 and 65) plus some N. lourensi WILDEKAMP, 1977 (see specimens of this locality on page 70). No other fishes were seen. All fishes were in good shape and condition. No measurements of the water of this locality were taken, but usually this type of habitat has very soft water with a low amount of salts and a pH of about 7 to 7.2.
Etymology: The specific name fuscotaeniatus is taken from the Latin fuscus, dark, and taenium, stripe, and refers to the dark bars across the body of especially the males but the females as well.
Distribution: Locality TZ 97/57 is the only place where this fish was collected, but the species is probably not restricted to this place and may occur in many mainly seasonal habitats in the (lower) Rufiji drainage, although this is an assumption only taken from the pattern of distribution of other Nothobranchius species as the syntopic collected N. lourensi.

Pachypanchax

Bis vor wenigen Jahren war über die Gattung relativ wenig bekannt. *Pachypanchax playfairii* war lange die einzige Art der Gattung, die in der Aquaristik vertreten war, zugleich ist dies ein recht harter Fisch, der auch für das Gesellschaftsbecken geeignet ist und so stets über die Jahre im Bestand erhalten wurde. Vorübergehend war auch ein oder zweimal ein Fisch von Madagaskar im Hobby, der als *P. omalonotus* angesprochen wurde. Erst in den letzten Jahren gelangten Formen dieser Gattung von Madagaskar zu uns, die eine gewisse Vielfalt deutlich werden ließen. Ob sie den von Madagaskar schon früher beschriebenen Arten *nuchisquamulatus* und *sakaramyi* zuzuordnen und ob diese beiden valide sind, ist gegenwärtig noch nicht geklärt, möglicherweise werden weitere Aufsammlungen noch eine größere Variabilität madegassischer Hechtlinge zutage fördern. Bisher wurde *nuchisquamulatus* als Synonym zu *omalonotus* betrachtet, solange keine weiteren gesicherten Informationen zu diesem Problem vorliegen, soll es hier bei dieser Zuordnung bleiben. Der in diesem Band als *sakaramyi* vorgestellte Fisch stammt vom Typenfundort der nominellen Art. Ob diese jedoch eigenständig ist, steht noch nicht fest, eventuell ist es nur eine Farbform von *P. omalonotus*. Alle bisher verfügbaren *Pachypanchax*-Populationen sind leicht zu pflegen und zur Fortpflanzung zu bringen. Ihr Verhalten entspricht dem von *Aplocheilus*- und robusten *Epiplatys*-Arten. Einzelne Tiere können, vor allem in nicht sehr großen Aquarien, auch gleichgroßen Mitbewohnern gegenüber recht ruppig sein.

Paranothobranchius

Paranothobranchius ocellatus, die einzige Art der Gattung, ist ökologisch mit *Belonesox belizanus* unter den Lebendgebärenden vergleichbar: Beide sind innerhalb ihrer Verwandtschaftsgruppe sehr groß und beide sind ausgesprochen räuberisch. *Paranothobranchius ocellatus* frißt alles was er bewältigen kann, und das sind nachgewiesenermaßen auch Fische von über 4 cm Länge. WILDEKAMP & HAAS (1992) sehen *Paranothobranchius* nicht als Gattung, sondern als Untergattung zu *Nothobranchius* und ordnen ihr gleichzeitig drei weitere Arten zu: *microlepis, fasciatus* und *bojiensis*. Doch wird diese Ansicht hier nicht geteilt, denn die Morphologie von *ocellatus* ist sehr abweichend (gestreckter Körper, spitzer Kopf mit langer Schnauze, zurückgestellte Dorsale und Anale), ferner auch die Färbung und Ökologie, all dies wird von den drei genannten Arten ebenso wie von anderen Arten der Gattung *Nothobranchius*, insbesondere in der Kombination, nicht geteilt.

Pronothobranchius kiyawensis

Pronothobranchius

Auch die Gattung *Pronothobranchius* ist monotypisch, ihr gehört nur eine einzige Art an: *Pronothobranchius kiyawensis*. Diese Art ist im Sahelbereich und der Guineasavanne weit verbreitet, von Senegambien im Westen bis zum Tschad-Einzug im Osten, nach Süden bis Südost-Ghana. In diesem Verbreitungsgebiet herrscht ein ausgesprochener Wechsel zwischen Regen- und Trockenzeit vor, und in Anpassung daran ist *P. kiyawensis* auch ein typischer Saisonfisch. Bei der Beschreibung der Art wurde diese von AHL der Gattung *Nothobranchius* zugeordnet. SCHEEL (1968) kannte noch keine lebenden Tiere, jedoch von der Beschreibung

All available Pachypanchaxes are easy to keep and to breed. They behave like Aplocheilus *or tough* Epiplatys *and larger specimens can be quite quarrelsome when kept in rather small tanks.*

Paranothobranchius

Paranothobranchius ocellatus, *the only species of the genus, can be - seen ecologically - compared with* Belonesox belizanus *from the Livebearer-group: both species are among the largest in their families and both are real predators.* Paranothobranchius ocellatus *eats simply everything that can be swallowed, even fish as large as 4 cm and over.* WILDEKAMP & HAAS (1992) *don't see* Paranothobranchius *as a separate genus but as a subgenus of* Nothobranchius *and assign three species to it: microlepis, fasciatus and bojiensis. I do not share this point of view, because the morphology (elongated body, pointed head with long snout, dorsal and anal fin placed more backwards) of* Paranothobranchius *is completely different from the three species mentioned above as well as from all other* Nothobranchius *species; also colouration and ecology are different, the combination of all three factors distinguishes the genus clearly from* Nothobranchius.

Paranothobranchius ocellatus

Pronothobranchius

The genus Pronothobranchius *is monotypical, too: the only species is* Pronothobranchius kiyawensis. *The species is widely distributed in the Sahel region and the savannas of Guinea, from Senegambia in the west to the drainage of Lake Chad in the east, and SE-Ghana in the south. In this particular distribution area, there is a distinct change of dry and wet season and, being perfectly adapted to this,* P. kiyawensis *is a typical seasonal fish. The first description of the species by* AHL *assigned it to the genus* Nothobranchius, *but in 1968, Scheel concluded from the type description (without having seen live specimens) that the species should be assigned to either* Aphyosemion *or* Fundulosoma, *not to* Nothobranchius. *In 1990, he classified* kiyawensis *as being definitely* Aphyosemion. PARENTI (1981) *regarded* Pronothobranchius *as a synonym of* Nothobranchius. P. kiyawensis *shares* Fundulosoma thierryi's *way of living, both species occur syntopic, i.e. they live in the same bodies of water.* P. kiyawensis *is a seasonal fish and bottom spawner which needs attentive care.*

Aphanius

SETHI (1960) *placed the genus* Aphanius *in a separate family, Aphaniidae, but usually the genus is regarded as belonging to the basically North American family Cyprinodontidae, its closest relatives. The genus* Aphanius *contains a group of killifishes that is probably very old in evolutionary terms and occurs in the drainages of the Mediterranean, Asia Minor and the Middle East as well as the Arabic Peninsula, especially the coastal drainages of the latter. To the south, it is distributed along the African horn, to the east as far as Pakistan. A kind of distributive centre can be found in Turkey. Altogether, the distribution area embraces the region that used to be the so-called Tethys, a prehistoric ocean dividing the connected northern*

der Typen her stellte er fest, daß die Art zu *Aphyosemion* oder vielleicht zu *Fundulosoma* zu stellen sei, nicht aber zu *Nothobranchius*, 1990 ordnete er *kiyawensis* eindeutig zu *Aphyosemion*. PARENTI (1981) sah *Pronothobranchius* als einfaches Synonym zu *Nothobranchius*.

Die Lebensweise von *P. kiyawensis* entspricht der von *Fundulosoma thierryi*, beide kommen an einigen Fundorten auch syntop vor, finden sich also gemeinsam im gleichen Gewässer. Auch *P. kiyawensis* ist ein Saisonfisch, der sich als Bodenlaicher fortpflanzt und schon einige Aufmerksamkeit in Haltung und Pflege erfordert.

Aphanius

SETHI (1960) stellte die Gattung *Aphanius* in eine eigene Familie Aphaniidae, vielfach wird sie aber immer noch der nordamerikanischen Familie Cyprinodontidae zugeordnet, ihren nächsten Verwandten. Die Gattung *Aphanius* umfaßt eine erdgeschichtlich vermutlich relativ alte Gruppe von Killifischen, die heute den engeren Mittelmeereinzug, Klein- und Vorderasien sowie die arabische Halbinsel und insbesondere deren Küsteneinzug besiedeln. Südwärts reicht das Verbreitungsgebiet um das Afrikanische Horn herum, ostwärts bis Pakistan. In der Türkei findet sich ein gewisser Verbreitungsschwerpunkt. Insgesamt umfaßt das Vorkommen einen Raum, der früher von der sogenannten Tethys eingenommen wurde, einem Ur-Ozean, der die damals noch zusammenhängenden Nordkontinente Eurasien und Nordamerika (= Laurasia) von den Südkontinenten (= Gondwana) trennte. Bemerkenswert ist, daß die meisten *Aphanius*-Arten sehr salztolerant oder gar salzliebend sind. Man findet sie nicht selten nicht nur in reinem Süß- oder Seewasser, sondern sogar in hypersalinen Gewässern, deren Salzkonzentration über dem von Seewasser liegt. Solche Biotope sind zum Beispiel abgeschnittene Meereslagunen oder Salinen. Auch diese Lebensweise zeigt Parallelen zu den nordamerikanischen *Cyprinodon*-Arten.

Mehrfach gab es Versuche einer Aufteilung der Gattung *Aphanius*. HOEDEMAN (1951) stellte die Arten *dispar* und *fasciatus* in eine eigene Gattung *Aphaniops*, für schuppenlose anatolische Formen wurde *Kosswigichthys* SÖZER, 1942 vorgeschlagen, der bauchflossenlose *apodus* wurde in *Tellia* GERVAIS, 1853 gestellt. Jedoch auch jüngere Versuche, *Kosswigichthys* erneut aufleben zu lassen (PARENTI, 1981), haben sich nicht durchgesetzt. Obgleich also die meisten *Aphanius*-Arten sehr verschiedenartige und darunter auch sehr ungünstige Lebensräume besiedeln, ist die Pflege in Gefangenschaft oft nicht einfach. Ein Salzzusatz hat sich in der Praxis meist als vorteilhaft erwiesen. Ferner kommen die *Aphanius*-Arten schwerpunktmäßig in Lebensräumen vor, die im Laufe des Jahres eine große Temperaturdifferenz aufweisen können. Die Fische sollten also im Winter deutlich kühlere Temperaturen erhalten als im Sommer.

Valencia

Valencia ist die zweite europäische Killifischgattung. Bisher sind nur zwei Arten bekanntgeworden: *Valencia hispanica* in Südost-Spanien und *V. letourneuxi* von der südgriechischen Halbinsel Peloponnes sowie von West-Griechenland und dem nördlich anschließenden Adria-Einzug einschließlich der Insel Korfu. Man muß also davon ausgehen, daß die heutige Gattung *Valencia* früher einmal ein größeres Verbreitungsgebiet einnahm und daß die beiden gegenwärtigen Vorkommen nur Relikte dieses ehemaligen Areals darstellen. Heute ist vor allem *V. hispanica* in seinem natürlichen Vorkommen stark gefährdet. PARENTI (1981) stellt die Gattung *Valencia* in eine eigene Familie Valenciidae, während man sie zuvor den *Fundulus*-Arten Nordamerikas nahestellte, die heute einer Familie Fundulidae zugeordnet werden. Wie eng die Bezüge zwischen *Valencia* und *Fundulus* in der Tat sind, mag die Beschreibung von *Valencia lozanoi* CARUANA, GÓMEZ & ARTAL, 1984 zeigen. Hierbei handelt es sich in Wirklichkeit um eine ausgesetzte Population von *Fundulus heteroclitus* (LINNAEUS, 1766), dessen Heimat eigentlich Nordamerika ist.

Aphanius fasciatus

continents Eurasia and North America (= Laurasia) and the southern continents (= Gondwana). Most interesting is the fact, that all Aphanius species tolerate salt or even prefer it. Not rarely, they can be found in pure fresh water or marine conditions, but also in hypersaline water where the salt percentage is even higher than in marine water. Biotopes with such water conditions can be, for example, isolated sea-lagoons or salines. These living circumstances show some parallels to those of the North American Cyprinodon species.

Repeatedly, there have been attempts to split up the genus Aphanius. HOEDEMAN (1951) placed the species dispar and fasciatus in the separate genus Aphaniops, Anatolian, scaleless species were assigned to Kosswigichthys SÖZER, 1942 and apodus (a species without pelvic fins) classified as belonging to Tellia GERVAIS, 1853. But all these as well as later attempts to revive Kosswigichthys (PARENTI, 1981) were not successful. Although in nature, most Aphanius species inhabit different and sometimes very demanding habitats, keeping them is not easy. Adding salt to the aquarium water has proved to be reasonable. Imitating the variation of temperature the animals have to endure in the wild, is also recommended; during the winter period, the water temperature should be considerably lower.

Valencia hispanica

Valencia

Valencia is the second genus of European killifishes. At the moment, only two species are known: Valencia hispanica from SE-Spain and Valencia letourneuxi that occurs in waters of the Greek island Peleponnes, western Greece and the adjacent northern drainages of the Adriatic Sea, including the island Korfu. One has to assume, that these two distribution areas are the remains of a once much larger territory. Especially V. hispanica is very much endangered in its natural environment.

PARENTI (1981) placed the genus Valencia in a separate family, Valenciidae, whereas in the past, the genus had been put beside some North American Fundulus species which are today assigned to the family Fundulidae. How closely related the genera Valencia and Fundulus really are, shows the description of Valencia lozanoi CARUANA, GOMEZ & ARTAL, 1984. This species is in fact a released population of Fundulus heteroclitus (LINNAEUS, 1766) that is endemic to North America.

Anhand der nachstehend aufgeführten Liste soll es dem Aquarianer erleichtert werden, in der Literatur unter anderen als den hier aufgelisteten Namen erscheinende Arten aufzufinden. Die linke Spalte beinhaltet den zu suchenden Namen einer Unterart, Art oder Gattung, rechts findet sich der hier verwendete Name. Diese Liste erhebt keineswegs Anspruch auf Vollständigkeit, ältere und gesicherte Synonyme sind in der Liste nicht aufgeführt. Siehe hierzu z.B. SEEGERS, 1986, 1988.

The following list was compiled in order to help hobbyists to find species that might have different names in aquatic literature. The left column contains names of the subspecies, species, or genus you are looking for, the right column contains the corresponding names used in this book. This list does not claim to be complete, older and certain synonyms are not included (for further information, please see SEEGERS, 1986, 1988).

azureus, Epiplatys	Epiplatys olbrechtsi "RL 56"
Aphyosemion abacinum	Diapteron abacinum
Aphyosemion bochtleri	Aphyosemion herzogi
Aphyosemion bualanum	
(sensu SCHEEL, 1968)	Aphyosemion elberti
Aphyosemion cyanostictum	Diapteron cyanostictum
Aphyosemion fulgens	Diapteron fulgens
Aphyosemion georgiae	Diapteron georgiae
Aphyosemion kribianum	Aphyosemion fallax
Aphyosemion melanopteron	Aphyosemion congicum
Aphyosemion microphtalmum	Aphyosemion escherichi
Aphyosemion nigrifluvi	Aphyosemion guignardi
Aphyosemion santaisabellae	Aphyosemion oeseri
Aphyosemion schwoiseri	Aphyosemion fallax
Aphyosemion simulans	Aphyosemion escherichi
Aplocheilichthys eduardensis	Aplocheilichthys vitschumbaensis
Aplocheilichthys erikae	Aplocheilichthys bukobanus
Aplocheilichthys meyburgi	Aplocheilichthys bukobanus
Aplocheilichthys schalleri	Aplocheilichthys hutereaui
Aplocheilus kirchmayeri	Aplocheilus blockii
banforensis, Roloffia	Aphyosemion guignardi
berkenkampi, Epiplatys	Epiplatys ansorgii
bochtleri, Aphyosemion	Aphyosemion herzogi
bualanum, Aphyosemion	
(sensu SCHEEL, 1968)	Aphyosemion elberti
Cynopanchax	Aplocheilichthys
Cynopanchax bukobanus	Aplocheilichthys bukobanus
eduardensis, Aplocheilichthys	Aplocheilichthys vitschumbaensis
Epiplatys azureus	Epiplatys olbrechtsi "RL 56"

Epiplatys fasciolatus puetzi	Epiplatys olbrechtsi "RL 86"
Epiplatys berkenkampi	Epiplatys ansorgii
Epiplatys neumanni	Epiplatys sangmelinensis neumanni
erikae, Aplocheilichthys	Aplocheilichthys bukobanus
fasciolatus puetzi, Epiplatys	Epiplatys olbrechtsi "RL 86"
kirchmayeri, Aplocheilus	Aplocheilus blockii
kribianum, Aphyosemion	Aphyosemion fallax
melanopteron, Aphyosemion	Aphyosemion congicum
meyburgi, Aplocheilichthys	Aplocheilichthys bukobanus
microphtalmum, Aphyosemion	Aphyosemion escherichi
neumanni, Epiplatys	Epiplatys sangmelinensis neumanni
nigrifluvi, Aphyosemion	Aphyosemion guignardi
Nothobranchius ocellatus	Paranothobranchius ocellatus
Pantanodon podoxys	Pantanodon stuhlmanni
podoxys, Pantanodon	Pantanodon stuhlmanni
puetzi, Epiplatys fasciolatus	Epiplatys olbrechtsi "RL 86"
Roloffia	von der Nomenklaturkommission verworfener Name, die Arten sind hier bis zu einer Gattungsrevision vorläufig in Aphyosemion eingeordnet / *This name has been suppressed by the Commission of Nomenclature, the species of this genus are included here provisionally in* Aphyosemion.
Roloffia banforensis	Aphyosemion guignardi
santaisabellae, Aphyosemion	Aphyosemion oeseri
schalleri, Aplocheilichthys	Aplocheilichthys hutereaui
schwoiseri, Aphyosemion	Aphyosemion fallax
simulans, Aphyosemion	Aphyosemion escherichi

Anmerkungen zum Bildteil:

Die Legenden zu den Bildern enthalten die folgenden Angaben:
- Die AQUALOG-Code-Nummer der Art, gefolgt vom vollständigen wissenschaftlichen Namen. Seine Bedeutung ist auf Seite 2 erläutert.
- Den deutschen / den englischen populären Namen, soweit vorhanden.
  "ABC 97/1" kennzeichnet den Fundortcode eines Sammlers. Dieser Fundort ist nicht selten in verschiedener Literatur (z.B. DKG-Journal), insbesondere aber in LANGTON (1996) aufgeschlüsselt, oft aber auch (noch) unbekannt. In jedem Fall sollte eine solche Fundortpopulation aber unbedingt rein erhalten und rein weitergezüchtet werden, denn sonst geht in der Aquaristik die Vielfalt der Fundortformen verloren und es bleibt nach einigen Jahren eine Einheitsform einer Art übrig, die mit den Ausgangspopulationen, wie sie in der Natur vorgefunden werden, nicht mehr viel gemein hat. Überdies hat sich hin und wieder gezeigt, daß zwei zunächst einer Art zugeordnete Fundortpopulationen sich später als getrennte Arten herausstellten.
- [T.t.] bedeutet: Diese Population stammt vom Typenfundort der Art.
- In der dritten Zeile sind die Fundorte der Population, soweit bekannt, angegeben. Hierzu gilt das oben Dargestellte:

Fundortpopulationen stets rein weiterzüchten, nie kreuzen !

- Die Kürzel in der dritten Zeile und die Bedeutungen der Piktogramme der vierten Zeile sind auf der vorderen inneren Umschlagklappe erläutert, ausgeklappt erlaubt sie einen unmittelbaren Vergleich.

Some notes concerning the tables:

The captions of the photos contain the following information:
- *The Aqualog code-number of the species, followed by the complete scientific name of the species. It is explained in detail on page 2.*
- *The German / English common names as far as available.*
  "ABC 97/1" designates the collecting code or collecting localities of the different collectors. Such codes are sometimes explained in various literature (as for example the DKG-Journal), but see especially Langton (1996). Some codes, however, are not yet published. In any case every population should be purely bred to avoid the loss of the variability of the different strains as they were found in the wild and to avoid the production of hybrids. There could be the danger that within some years the variability of a given species might vanish and then there would only be a type in the hobby which has only little similarity with the wild strain.
- *[T.t.] means: This population originates from the type locality of the species.*
- *The collecting localities of the respective populations, as far as known, are given in the third line. Please remember:*

Do never interbreed specimens of different localities !

- *The abbreviations and ideograms of the third and fourth line are explained on the inside of the back cover, please, unfold it.*

Aplocheilidae BLEEKER, 1860

Aplocheilus McCLELLAND, 1839
A. blockii (ARNOLD, 1911)
A. dayi dayi (STEINDACHNER, 1892)
A. dayi werneri MEINKEN, 1966
A. lineatus (VALENCIENNES in CUVIER & VALENCIENNES, 1846)
A. panchax (HAMILTON, 1822)
A. parvus (RAJ, 1916)

Diapteron HUBER & SEEGERS, 1977
D. abacinum (HUBER, 1986)
D. cyanostictum (LAMBERT & GÉRY, 1967)
D. fulgens (RADDA, 1975)
D. georgiae (LAMBERT & GÉRY, 1967)
D. seegersi (HUBER, 1980)

Epiplatys GILL, 1862
E. (Pseudepiplatys) annulatus (BOULENGER, 1915)
E. ansorgii (BOULENGER, 1911)
E. barmoiensis SCHEEL, 1968
E. biafranus RADDA, 1970
E. bifasciatus (STEINDACHNER, 1881)
E. boulengeri (PELLEGRIN, 1926)
E. chaperi chaperi (SAUVAGE, 1882)
E. chaperi schreiberi BERKENKAMP, 1975
E. chaperi sheljuzhkoi POLL, 1953
E. chevalieri (PELLEGRIN, 1904)
E. coccinatus BERKENKAMP & ETZEL, 1982 (= E. ruhkopfi?)
E. dageti dageti POLL, 1953
E. dageti monroviae ARNOULT & DAGET, 1964
E. esekanus SCHEEL, 1968
E. fasciolatus fasciolatus (GÜNTHER, 1866)
E. fasciolatus tototaensis ROMAND, 1978
E. fasciolatus zimiensis BERKENKAMP, 1977
E. grahami (BOULENGER, 1911)
E. guineensis ROMAND, 1994
E. hildegardae BERKENKAMP, 1983
E. huberi (RADDA & PÜRZL, 1981)
E. lamottei DAGET, 1954
E. longiventralis (BOULENGER, 1911)
E. mesogramma HUBER, 1980
E. multifasciatus (BOULENGER, 1913)
E. njalaensis NEUMANN, 1976
E. olbrechtsi olbrechtsi POLL, 1941
E. olbrechtsi dauresi ROMAND, 1985
E. olbrechtsi kassiapleuensis BERKENKAMP & ETZEL, 1977
E. olbrechtsi puetzi BERKENKAMP & ETZEL, 1985
E. phoeniceps HUBER, 1980
E. roloffi ROMAND, 1978
E. ruhkopfi BERKENKAMP & ETZEL, 1980
E. sangmelinensis neumanni BERKENKAMP, 1993
E. sangmelinensis sangmelinensis (AHL, 1928)
E. sexfasciatus sexfasciatus GILL, 1862
E. sexfasciatus baroi BERKENKAMP, 1975
E. sexfasciatus rathkei RADDA, 1970
E. sexfasciatus togolensis LOISELLE, 1970
E. singa (BOULENGER, 1899)
E. spilargyreius (DUMÉRIL, 1861)

Episemion RADDA & PÜRZL, 1987
E. callipteron RADDA & PÜRZL, 1987

Foerschichthys SCHEEL & ROMAND, 1981
F. flavipinnis (MEINKEN, 1932)

Fundulosoma AHL, 1924
F. thierryi AHL, 1924

* In der Reihenfolge der Fotos im Bildteil /
* In the same order as in the photo section

Nothobranchius PETERS, 1868
N. bojiensis WILDEKAMP & HAAS, 1992
N. brieni POLL, 1938
N. eggersi SEEGERS, 1982
N. elongatus WILDEKAMP, 1982
N. fasciatus WILDEKAMP & HAAS, 1992
N. foerschi WILDEKAMP & BERKENKAMP, 1979
N. furzeri JUBB, 1971
N. fuscotaeniatus SEEGERS, 1997
N. guentheri (PFEFFER, 1893)
N. interruptus WILDEKAMP & BERKENKAMP, 1979
N. janpapi WILDEKAMP, 1977
N. jubbi WILDEKAMP & BERKENKAMP, 1979
N. kafuensis WILDEKAMP & ROSENSTOCK, 1989
N. kirki JUBB, 1969
N. korthausae MEINKEN, 1973
N. kuhntae (AHL, 1926)
N. lourensi WILDEKAMP, 1977
N. luekei SEEGERS, 1984
N. malaissei WILDEKAMP, 1978
N. melanospilus (PFEFFER, 1896)
N. microlepis (VINCIGUERRA, 1897)
N. neumanni (HILGENDORF, 1905)
N. orthonotus (PETERS, 1844)
N. palmqvisti (LÖNNBERG, 1907)
N. patrizii (VINCIGUERRA, 1927)
N. polli WILDEKAMP, 1978
N. rachovii AHL, 1926
N. robustus AHL, 1935
N. rubripinnis SEEGERS, 1986
N. rubroreticulatus BLACHE & MITON, 1960
N. steinforti WILDEKAMP, 1977
N. symoensi WILDEKAMP, 1978
N. taeniopygus HILGENDORF, 1891
N. willerti WILDEKAMP, 1992
N. virgatus CHAMBERS, 1984
N. vossleri AHL, 1924

Pachypanchax MYERS, 1933
P. omalonotus (DUMÉRIL, 1861)
P. playfairii (GÜNTHER, 1866)
P. sakaramyi (HOLLY, 1928)

Paranothobranchius SEEGERS, 1985
P. ocellatus SEEGERS, 1985

Pronothobranchius RADDA, 1969
P. kiyawensis (AHL, 1928)

Aphaniidae SETHI, 1960

Aphanius NARDO, 1827
A. anatoliae anatoliae (LEIDENFROST, 1912)
A. anatoliae splendens (KOSSWIG & SÖZER, 1945)
A. anatoliae sureyanus (NEU, 1937)
A. anatoliae transgrediens (ERMIN, 1946)
A. (Tellia) apodus (GERVAIS, 1853)
A. (Kosswigichthys) asquamatus (SÖZER, 1942)
A. chantrei (GAILLARD, 1895)
A. dispar dispar (RÜPPELL, 1829)
A. dispar richardsoni (BOULENGER, 1907)
A. fasciatus (VALENCIENNES in HUMBOLDT & VALENCIENNES, 1821)
A. ginaonis (HOLLY, 1929)
A. iberus (VALENCIENNES in CUVIER & VALENCIENNES, 1846)
A. mento (HECKEL in RUSSEGGER, 1843)
A. sirhani VILLWOCK, SCHOLL & KRUPP, 1983
A. sophiae (HECKEL in RUSSEGGER, 1846)
A. vladykovi COAD, 1988

Valenciidae PARENTI, 1981

Valencia MYERS, 1928
V. hispanica (VALENCIENNES in CUVIER & VALENCIENNES, 1846)
V. letourneuxi (SAUVAGE, 1880)

Photo: O. Roth

Aplocheilidae
Asiatische Arten

1. Sri Lanka, Bentota-Fluß südlich von Ittapana. Vorkommen von *Aplocheilus dayi*.
2. Westküste von Malaysia, Kuala Terong. Fundort von *Aplocheilus panchax*, Barben, einem Prachtzwerggurami und Halbschnabelhechtlingen.
3. Sri Lanka, Anguruwatota, Kottawa Forest. Reisfelder mit *Aplocheilus parvus* und *Pseudosphromenus cupanus*.

Photo: O. Roth

1. Sri Lanka, Bentota River south of Ittapana. Habitat of *Aplocheilus dayi*.
2. Malaysian westcoast, Kuala Terong. Here *Aplocheilus panchax*, barbs, a licorice gourami and halfbeaks were collected.
3. Sri Lanka, Anguruwatota, Kottawa Forest. Paddies with *Aplocheilus parvus* and *Pseudosphromenus cupanus*.

Photo: O. Roth

X07005-4 *Aplocheilus blockii* (ARNOLD, 1911)
Vorderindischer Zwerghechtling / Green Panchax
Wirakateya, Sri Lanka or Ceylon; W; 5 cm

▷ ♗ ◑ ☺ ☻ ⬆ 🖼 ➥ ⚠ Ⓢ Ⓜ ♂

Photo: L. Seegers

X07005-4 *Aplocheilus blockii* (ARNOLD, 1911)
Vorderindischer Zwerghechtling / Green Panchax
Wirakateya, Sri Lanka or Ceylon; W; 5 cm

▷ ♗ ◑ ☺ ☻ ⬆ 🖼 ➥ ⚠ Ⓢ Ⓜ ♂

Photo: L. Seegers

X07006-4 *Aplocheilus blockii* (ARNOLD, 1911)
Vorderindischer Zwerghechtling / Green Panchax
Kottawa Forest, Sri Lanka or Ceylon; W; 5 cm

▷ ♗ ◑ ☺ ☻ ⬆ 🖼 ➥ ⚠ Ⓢ Ⓜ ♂

Photo: L. Seegers

X07007-4 *Aplocheilus blockii* (ARNOLD, 1911)
Vorderindischer Zwerghechtling / Green Panchax
Colva Beach, Goa, Indien / India; W; 5 cm

▷ ♗ ◑ ☺ ☻ ⬆ 🖼 ➥ ⚠ Ⓢ Ⓜ ♂

Photo: L. Seegers

X07007-4 *Aplocheilus blockii* (ARNOLD, 1911)
Vorderindischer Zwerghechtling / Green Panchax
Colva Beach, Goa, Indien / India; W; 5 cm

▷ ♗ ◑ ☺ ☻ ⬆ 🖼 ➥ ⚠ Ⓢ Ⓜ ♂

Photo: L. Seegers

X07007-4 *Aplocheilus blockii* (ARNOLD, 1911)
Vorderindischer Zwerghechtling / Green Panchax
Colva Beach, Goa, Indien / India; W; 5 cm

▷ ♗ ◑ ☺ ☻ ⬆ 🖼 ➥ ⚠ Ⓢ Ⓜ ♀

Photo: L. Seegers

X07007-4 *Aplocheilus blockii* (ARNOLD, 1911)
Vorderindischer Zwerghechtling / Green Panchax
Colva Beach, Goa, Indien / India; W; 5 cm

▷ ♗ ◑ ☺ ☻ ⬆ 🖼 ➥ ⚠ Ⓢ Ⓜ ♂

Photo: L. Seegers

X07007-4 *Aplocheilus blockii* (ARNOLD, 1911)
Vorderindischer Zwerghechtling / Green Panchax
Colva Beach, Goa, Indien / India; W; 5 cm

▷ ♗ ◑ ☺ ☻ ⬆ 🖼 ➥ ⚠ Ⓢ Ⓜ ♀

Photo: L. Seegers

X07010-4 *Aplocheilus dayi dayi* (STEINDACHNER, 1892)
Grüner Streifenhechtling / Ceylonese Panchax, Day's Panchax
Aquaristikimport, Sri Lanka / Aquarium Import, Sri Lanka; W; 9-10 cm
▷♫➊☺☹⊞▦➤ ◈▣ ♂   Photo: L. Seegers

X07010-4 *Aplocheilus dayi dayi* (STEINDACHNER, 1892)
Grüner Streifenhechtling / Ceylonese Panchax, Day's Panchax
Aquaristikimport, Sri Lanka / Aquarium Import, Sri Lanka; W; 9-10 cm
▷♫➊☺☹⊞▦➤ ◈▣ ♀   Photo: L. Seegers

X07011-4 *Aplocheilus dayi werneri* MEINKEN, 1966
Grüner Streifenhechtling / Ceylonese Panchax, Day's Panchax
Kottawa Forest, Sri Lanka or Ceylon; W; 9 cm
▷♫➊☺☹⊞▦➤ ◈▣ ♂   Photo: L. Seegers

X07011-4 *Aplocheilus dayi werneri* MEINKEN, 1966
Grüner Streifenhechtling / Ceylonese Panchax, Day's Panchax
Kottawa Forest, Sri Lanka or Ceylon; W; 9 cm
▷♫➊☺☹⊞▦➤ ◈▣ ♀   Photo: L. Seegers

X07011-4 *Aplocheilus dayi werneri* MEINKEN, 1966
Grüner Streifenhechtling / Ceylonese Panchax, Day's Panchax
Kottawa Forest, Sri Lanka or Ceylon; W; 9 cm
▷♫➊☺☹⊞▦➤ ◈▣ ♂   Photo: L. Seegers

X07023-4 *Aplocheilus lineatus* VALENCIENNES in CUVIER & VALENCIENNES,
Streifenhechtling / Striped Panchax   1846
20 km after Mayemlake, N Goa, SW India; B; 10 cm
▷♫➊☺☹⊞▦➤ ◈▣ ♂   Photo: L. Seegers

X07024-4 *Aplocheilus lineatus* VALENCIENNES in CUVIER & VALENCIENNES,
Streifenhechtling / Striped Panchax   1846
Sanquelin, Indien / Sanquelin, India; B; 10 cm
▷♫➊☺☹⊞▦➤ ◈▣ ♂   Photo: L. Seegers

X07024-4 *Aplocheilus lineatus* VALENCIENNES in CUVIER & VALENCIENNES,
Streifenhechtling / Striped Panchax   1846
Sanquelin, Indien / Sanquelin, India; B; 10 cm
▷♫➊☺☹⊞▦➤ ◈▣ ♀   Photo: L. Seegers

X07020-4 *Aplocheilus lineatus* VALENCIENNES in CUVIER & VALENCIENNES, 1846   Photo: H.J. Mayland
Streifenhechtling / Striped Panchax
Aquarienstamm / Aquarium strain; B; 10 cm
▷ ♫ ◑ ☺ ☹ ⊞ ▦ ➤ ◈ ▥ ♂

X07021-4 *Aplocheilus lineatus* VALENCIENNES in CUVIER & VALENCIENNES,
Goldener Streifenhechtling / Golden Striped Panchax   1846
Aquarienstamm / Aquarium strain; Z; 10 cm
▷ ♫ ◑ ☺ ☹ ⊞ ▦ ➤ ◈ ▥ ♂   Photo: L. Seegers

X07020-4 *Aplocheilus lineatus* VALENCIENNES in CUVIER & VALENCIENNES,
Streifenhechtling / Striped Panchax   1846
Aquarienstamm / Aquarium strain; B; 10 cm
▷ ♫ ◑ ☺ ☹ ⊞ ▦ ➤ ◈ ▥ ♂   Photo: F. Vermeulen

X07025-4 *Aplocheilus lineatus* VALENCIENNES in CUVIER & VALENCIENNES,
"Smaragd"-Streifenhechtling / "Smaragd" Striped Panchax   1846
Aquarienstamm / Aquarium strain; Z; 10 cm
▷ ♫ ◑ ☺ ☹ ⊞ ▦ ➤ ◈ ▥ ♂   Photo: L. Seegers

X07025-4 *Aplocheilus lineatus* VALENCIENNES in CUVIER & VALENCIENNES,
"Smaragd"-Streifenhechtling / "Smaragd" Striped Panchax   1846
Aquarienstamm / Aquarium strain; Z; 10 cm
▷ ♫ ◑ ☺ ☹ ⊞ ▦ ➤ ◈ ▥ ♀   Photo: L. Seegers

X07046-4 *Aplocheilus panchax* (HAMILTON-BUCHANAN, 1822)
Panchax, Gemeiner Hechtling / Panchax
Kalkutta, Indien / Calcutta, India; W; 8 cm
▷ℬ◑☺☹⬆🖼➡ ◈m ♂
Photo: L. Seegers

X07046-4 *Aplocheilus panchax* (HAMILTON-BUCHANAN, 1822)
Panchax, Gemeiner Hechtling / Panchax
Kalkutta, Indien / Calcutta, India; W; 8 cm
▷ℬ◑☺☹⬆🖼➡ ◈m ♀
Photo: L. Seegers

X07047-4 *Aplocheilus panchax* (HAMILTON-BUCHANAN, 1822)
Panchax, Gemeiner Hechtling / Panchax
Dalwar, Indien / Dalwar, India; W; 8 cm
▷ℬ◑☺☹⬆🖼➡ ◈m ♂
Photo: L. Seegers

X07048-4 *Aplocheilus panchax* (HAMILTON-BUCHANAN, 1822)
Panchax, Gemeiner Hechtling / Panchax
Indien / India; W; 8 cm
▷ℬ◑☺☹⬆🖼➡ ◈m ♂
Photo: L. Seegers

X07049-4 *Aplocheilus panchax* (HAMILTON-BUCHANAN, 1822)
Panchax, Gemeiner Hechtling / Panchax
Phuket, Thailand; W; 8 cm
▷ℬ◑☺☹⬆🖼➡ ◈m ♂
Photo: L. Seegers

X07050-4 *Aplocheilus panchax* (HAMILTON-BUCHANAN, 1822)
Panchax, Gemeiner Hechtling / Panchax
Tioman; W; 8 cm
▷ℬ◑☺☹⬆🖼➡ ◈m ♂
Photo: L. Seegers

X07051-4 *Aplocheilus panchax* (HAMILTON-BUCHANAN, 1822)
Panchax, Gemeiner Hechtling / Panchax
Chao Phaya River, Thailand; W; 8 cm
▷ℬ◑☺☹⬆🖼➡ ◈m ♂
Photo: L. Seegers

X07051-4 *Aplocheilus panchax* (HAMILTON-BUCHANAN, 1822)
Panchax, Gemeiner Hechtling / Panchax
Chao Phaya River, Thailand; W; 8 cm
▷ℬ◑☺☹⬆🖼➡ ◈m ♀
Photo: L. Seegers

X07052-4 *Aplocheilus panchax* (Hamilton-Buchanan, 1822)
Panchax, Gemeiner Hechtling / Panchax
Bali, Indonesien / Bali, Indonesia; W; 8 cm
Photo: L. Seegers

X07053-4 *Aplocheilus panchax* (Hamilton-Buchanan, 1822)
Panchax, Gemeiner Hechtling / Panchax
Bukittinggi, West-Sumatra / Western Sumatra; W; 8 cm
Photo: L. Seegers

X07045-4 *Aplocheilus panchax* (Hamilton-Buchanan, 1822)
Panchax, Gemeiner Hechtling / Panchax
Aquarienstamm / Aquarium strain; W; 8 cm
Photo: L. Seegers

X07045-4 *Aplocheilus panchax* (Hamilton-Buchanan, 1822)
Panchax, Gemeiner Hechtling / Panchax
Aquarienstamm / Aquarium strain; W; 8 cm
Photo: L. Seegers

X07060-4 *Aplocheilus parvus* (Raj, 1916)
Zwerghechtling / Dwarf Panchax
Aquarienstamm / Aquarium strain; B; 5 cm
Photo: L. Seegers

X07061-4 *Aplocheilus parvus* (Raj, 1916)
Zwerghechtling / Dwarf Panchax
Sri Lanka oder Ceylon /Sri Lanka or Ceylon; W; 5 cm
Photo: L. Seegers

X07062-4 *Aplocheilus parvus* (Raj, 1916)
Zwerghechtling / Dwarf Panchax
Kalutara, Indien / Kalutara, India; B; 5 cm
Photo: L. Seegers

X07062-4 *Aplocheilus parvus* (Raj, 1916)
Zwerghechtling / Dwarf Panchax
Kalutara, Indien / Kalutara, India; B; 5 cm
Photo: L. Seegers

© Verlag A.C.S. GmbH

Aplocheilidae
Afrikanische Arten

Photo: E. Pürzl

1. Fundort von *Diapteron cyanostictum* und *D. georgiae* östlich von Ovan, Gabun.
2. *Diapteron cyanostictum* kamen auch an dieser Stelle in der Umgebung von Ovan, Gabun, vor.

1. Collecting locality of *Diapteron cyanostictum* and *D. georgiae* east of Ovan, Gabon.
2. From this place near Ovan, Gabon, *Diapteron cyanostictum* was collected.

Photo: E. Pürzl

A29350-4 *Diapteron abacinum* (Huber, 1976)
Mékambo-Zwergprachtkärpfling / Mékambo Dwarf Killi [T.t.]
30 km NO Mékambo, Gabun / Gabon; W; 3,5 cm

Photo: L. Seegers

A29351-4 *Diapteron abacinum* (Huber, 1976)
Mékambo-Zwergprachtkärpfling / Mékambo Dwarf Killi
Makokou, Gabun / Gabon; W; 3,5 cm

Photo: L. Seegers

A29352-4 *Diapteron abacinum* (Huber, 1976)
Mékambo-Zwergprachtkärpfling / Mékambo Dwarf Killi
Gabun / Gabon; B; 3,5 cm

Photo: R. Lütje

A29355-3 *Diapteron cyanostictum* (Lambert & Géry, 1967)
Blaupunkt-Zwergprachtkärpfling / Blue Spotted Dwarf Killi "GBN 88/28"
Gabun / Gabon; W; 3 cm

Photo: S. Hellner-

A29356-4 *Diapteron cyanostictum* (Lambert & Géry, 1967)
Blaupunkt-Zwergprachtkärpfling / Blue Spotted Dwarf Killi
Makokou, Gabun / Makokou, Gabon; W; 3 cm

Photo: L. Seegers

A29355-3 *Diapteron cyanostictum* (Lambert & Géry, 1967)
Blaupunkt-Zwergprachtkärpfling / Blue Spotted Dwarf Killi "GBN 88/29"
Gabun / Gabon; W; 3 cm

Photo: S. Hellner-

A29357-4 *Diapteron cyanostictum* (Lambert & Géry, 1967)
Blaupunkt-Zwergprachtkärpfling / Blue Spotted Dwarf Killi
30 km W Makokou, Gabun / Gabon; B; 3 cm

Photo: L. Seegers

A29357-4 *Diapteron cyanostictum* (Lambert & Géry, 1967)
Blaupunkt-Zwergprachtkärpfling / Blue Spotted Dwarf Killi
30 km W Makokou, Gabun / Gabon; B; 3 cm

Photo: L. Seegers

A29360-4 *Diapteron fulgens* (RADDA, 1975)
Orange-Zwergprachtkärpfling / Orange Dwarf Killi
30 km W Makokou, Gabun / Gabon; W; 3,5 cm

Photo: L. Seegers

A29360-4 *Diapteron fulgens* (RADDA, 1975)
Orange-Zwergprachtkärpfling / Orange Dwarf Killi
30 km W Makokou, Gabun / Gabon; W; 3,5 cm

Photo: L. Seegers

A29360-4 *Diapteron fulgens* (RADDA, 1975)
Orange-Zwergprachtkärpfling / Orange Dwarf Killi
30 km W Makokou, Gabun / Gabon; W; 3,5 cm

Photo: L. Seegers

A29360-4 *Diapteron fulgens* (RADDA, 1975)
Orange-Zwergprachtkärpfling / Orange Dwarf Killi
30 km W Makokou, Gabun / Gabon; W; 3,5 cm

Photo: L. Seegers

A29360-4 *Diapteron fulgens* (RADDA, 1975)
Orange-Zwergprachtkärpfling / Orange Dwarf Killi
30 km W Makokou, Gabun / Gabon; W; 3,5 cm

Photo: L. Seegers

A29360-4 *Diapteron fulgens* (Radda, 1975)
Orange-Zwergprachtkärpfling / Orange Dwarf Killi
30 km W Makokou, Gabun / Gabon; W; 3,5 cm

◁ ▷ 🦟 ◑ ☺ 🔲 🖼 ➤ ⚠ Ⓢ ♂ Photo: L. Seegers

A29360-4 *Diapteron fulgens* (Radda, 1975)
Orange-Zwergprachtkärpfling / Orange Dwarf Killi
30 km W Makokou, Gabun / Gabon; W; 3,5 cm

◁ ▷ 🦟 ◑ ☺ 🔲 🖼 ➤ ⚠ Ⓢ ♀ Photo: L. Seegers

A29361-4 *Diapteron fulgens* (Radda, 1975)
Orange-Zwergprachtkärpfling / Orange Dwarf Killi, "GWW 86/6"
Gabun / Gabon; B; 3,5 cm

◁ ▷ 🦟 ◑ ☺ 🔲 🖼 ➤ ⚠ Ⓢ ♂ Photo: S. Hellner

A29361-4 *Diapteron fulgens* (Radda, 1975)
Orange-Zwergprachtkärpfling / Orange Dwarf Killi
Gabun / Gabon; B; 3,5 cm

◁ ▷ 🦟 ◑ ☺ 🔲 🖼 ➤ ⚠ Ⓢ ♂ Photo: R. Lütje

A29370-4 *Diapteron georgiae* (Lambert & Géry, 1967)
Georgias Zwergprachtkärpfling / Georgia's Spotted Dwarf Killi
70 km W Makokou, Gabun / Gabon; B; 3,5 cm

◁ ▷ 🦟 ◑ ☺ 🔲 🖼 ➤ ⚠ Ⓢ ♂ Photo: L. Seegers

A29370-4 *Diapteron georgiae* (Lambert & Géry, 1967)
Georgias Zwergprachtkärpfling / Georgia's Spotted Dwarf Killi
70 km W Makokou, Gabun / Gabon; B; 3,5 cm

◁ ▷ 🦟 ◑ ☺ 🔲 🖼 ➤ ⚠ Ⓢ ♀ Photo: L. Seegers

A29371-4 *Diapteron georgiae* (Lambert & Géry, 1967)
Georgias Zwergprachtkärpfling / Georgia's Spotted Dwarf Killi
"GWW 86/2", Gabun / Gabon; B; 3,5 cm

◁ ▷ 🦟 ◑ ☺ 🔲 🖼 ➤ ⚠ Ⓢ ♂ Photo: S. Hellner

A29371-4 *Diapteron georgiae* (Lambert & Géry, 1967)
Georgias Zwergprachtkärpfling / Georgia's Spotted Dwarf Killi
Umgebung von Makokou, Gabun / Makokou area, Gabon; B; 3,5 cm

◁ ▷ 🦟 ◑ ☺ 🔲 🖼 ➤ ⚠ Ⓢ ♂ Photo: L. Seegers

Photo: E. Pürzl

Photo: E. Pürzl

Photo: E. Pürzl

1. Fundort von *Epiplatys singa* bei Boma in Zaïre oder Kongo.
2. Hier wurde *Epiplatys multifasciatus* gefangen (Kongo Fluß in Zaïre oder Kongo).
3. Dieser Bach bei Tabou in der westlichen Elfenbeinküste ist Lebensraum von *Epiplatys dageti*.

1. *At this place near Boma in Zaïre or Kongo* Epiplatys singa *was collected.*
2. *Collecting locality of* Epiplatys multifasciatus *at the border of the Kongo River in Zaïre or Kongo.*
3. *This brook near Tabou in western Ivory Coast is the habitat of* Epiplatys dageti.

A76655-4 *Epiplatys (Pseudepiplatys) annulatus* (Boulenger, 1915)
Ringelhechtling / Clown Killifish
Aquarienstamm /Aquarium strain; B; 3,5 cm

⚠🕭◑☺🔼🖼️🐟 ⚠ Ⓢ⒮ Ⓢ♂ Photo: L. Seegers

A76656-4 *Epiplatys (Pseudepiplatys) annulatus* (Boulenger, 1915)
Ringelhechtling / Clown Killifish
Monrovia, Liberia; W; 3,5 cm

⚠🕭◑☺🔼🖼️🐟 ⚠ Ⓢ⒮ Ⓢ♂ Photo: L. Seegers

A76657-4 *Epiplatys (Pseudepiplatys) annulatus* (Boulenger, 1915)
Ringelhechtling / Clown Killifish
Sowoja River, Sierra Leone "SL 89"; W; 3,5 cm

⚠🕭◑☺🔼🖼️🐟 ⚠ Ⓢ⒮ Ⓢ♂ Photo: S. Hellner

A76655-4 *Epiplatys (Pseudepiplatys) annulatus* (Boulenger, 1915)
Ringelhechtling / Clown Killifish
Aquarienstamm / Aquarium strain; B; 3,5 cm

⚠🕭◑☺🔼🖼️🐟 ⚠ Ⓢ⒮ Ⓢ♀ Photo: H.-G. Evers

A30800-4 *Epiplatys ansorgii* (Boulenger, 1911)
Ansorges Hechtling / Ansorge's Panchax
30 km S Lambarene on Bigouenia - Mora road, Gabon; B; 7,5 cm

▷🕭◑☺☹🔼🖼️🐟 ◈🔟 ♂ Photo: L. Seegers

A30800-4 *Epiplatys ansorgii* (Boulenger, 1911)
Ansorges Hechtling / Ansorge's Panchax
30 km S Lambarene on Bigouenia - Mora road, Gabon; B; 7,5 cm

▷🕭◑☺☹🔼🖼️🐟 ◈🔟 ♀ Photo: L. Seegers

A30801-4 *Epiplatys ansorgii* (Boulenger, 1911)
Ansorges Hechtling / Ansorge's Panchax
Gamba, Gabun / Gabon; B; 7,5 cm

▷🕭◑☺☹🔼🖼️🐟 ◈🔟 ♂ Photo: L. Seegers

A30801-4 *Epiplatys ansorgii* (Boulenger, 1911)
Ansorges Hechtling / Ansorge's Panchax
Gamba, Gabun / Gabon; B; 7,5 cm

▷🕭◑☺☹🔼🖼️🐟 ◈🔟 ♀ Photo: H.-G. Evers

A30802-3 *Epiplatys ansorgii* (Boulenger, 1911)
Ansorges Hechtling / Ansorge's Panchax
Gabun / Gabon; B; 7,5 cm
▷♫◑☺☹⊞🖼🦐 ◈ⅿ♂
Photo: L. Seegers

A30803-4 *Epiplatys ansorgii* (Boulenger, 1911)
Ansorges Hechtling / Ansorge's Panchax
Sindara, Gabun / Gabon; B; 7,5 cm
▷♫◑☺☹⊞🖼🦐 ◈ⅿ♂
Photo: H.-G. Evers

A30803-4 *Epiplatys ansorgii* (Boulenger, 1911)
Ansorges Hechtling / Ansorge's Panchax
Sindara, Gabun / Gabon; B; 7,5 cm
▷♫◑☺☹⊞🖼🦐 ◈ⅿ♂
Photo: E. Pürzl

A30805-4 *Epiplatys* sp. aff. *ansorgii* (Boulenger, 1911)
Ansorges Hechtling / Ansorge's Panchax
Mayumba, Gabun / Gabon; W; 10 cm
▷♫◑☺☹⊞🖼🦐 ◈ⅿ♂
Photo: E. Pürzl

A30810-4 *Epiplatys barmoiensis* Scheel, 1968
Barmoi-Hechtling / Barmoi Panchax
Rokupr Pump Station, Sierra Leone; B; 7,0 cm
⚠♫◑☺☹⊞🖼🦐 ◈ⅿ♂ (front) ♀
Photo: S. Hellner

A30811-4 *Epiplatys barmoiensis* Scheel, 1968
Barmoi-Hechtling / Barmoi Panchax
Elfenbeinküste / Ivory Coast; W; 7,0 cm
⚠♫◑☺☹⊞🖼🦐 ◈ⅿ♂
Photo: L. Seegers

A30812-4 *Epiplatys barmoiensis* Scheel, 1968
Barmoi-Hechtling / Barmoi Panchax
Liberia; B; 7,0 cm
⚠♫◑☺☹⊞🖼🦐 ◈ⅿ♂
Photo: H.-G. Evers

A30812-4 *Epiplatys barmoiensis* Scheel, 1968
Barmoi-Hechtling / Barmoi Panchax
Liberia; B; 7,0 cm
⚠♫◑☺☹⊞🖼🦐 ◈ⅿ ♀
Photo: H.-G. Evers

A30813-4 *Epiplatys barmoiensis* SCHEEL, 1968
Barmoi-Hechtling / Barmoi Panchax
Aquaristikimport von Nigeria / Aquarium import from Nigeria; W; 7,0 cm

Photo: L. Seegers

A30814-4 *Epiplatys barmoiensis* SCHEEL, 1968
Barmoi-Hechtling / Barmoi Panchax
Aquarienstamm / Aquarium strain; B; 7,0 cm

Photo: E. Pürzl

A30820-4 *Epiplatys biafranus* RADDA, 1970
Biafra-Hechtling / Biafra Panchax
Isiokpo, Nigeria; B; 5,0 cm

Photo: L. Seegers

A30821-4 *Epiplatys biafranus* RADDA, 1970
Biafra-Hechtling / Biafra Panchax
Aba, Nigeria; W; 5,0 cm

Photo: E. Pürzl

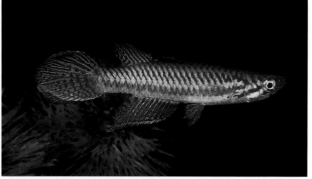

A30825-4 *Epiplatys bifasciatus* (STEINDACHNER, 1881)
Zweistreifen-Hechtling / Twostriped Panchax
Abuko, Gambia; W; 5,0 cm

Photo: L. Seegers

A30826-4 *Epiplatys bifasciatus* (STEINDACHNER, 1881)
Zweistreifen-Hechtling / Twostriped Panchax
Bwian, Gambia; W; 5,0 cm

Photo: L. Seegers

A30827-4 *Epiplatys bifasciatus* (STEINDACHNER, 1881)
Zweistreifen-Hechtling / Twostriped Panchax
Mali; W; 5,0 cm

Photo: L. Seegers

A30828-3 *Epiplatys bifasciatus* (STEINDACHNER, 1881)
Zweistreifen-Hechtling / Twostriped Panchax
Bormako Lida, Mali; B; 5,0 cm

Photo: H.-G. Evers

© Verlag A.C.S. GmbH

A30829-4 *Epiplatys bifasciatus* (Steindachner, 1881)
Zweistreifen-Hechtling / Twostriped Panchax
Guinea; B; 5,0 cm

▷△♬◑☺☺⊕⊞🖼➡ ◈🔲♂
Photo: H.-G. Evers

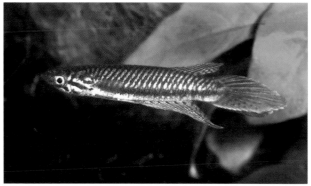

A30830-4 *Epiplatys bifasciatus* (Steindachner, 1881)
Zweistreifen-Hechtling / Twostriped Panchax
Aquaristik-Import / Aquarium import, Guinea; W; 5,0 cm

▷△♬◑☺☺⊕⊞🖼➡ ◈🔲♂
Photo: L. Seegers

A30831-4 *Epiplatys bifasciatus* (Steindachner, 1881)
Zweistreifen-Hechtling / Twostriped Panchax
Malal, Sierra Leone, "SL 89"; B; 5,0 cm

▷△♬◑☺☺⊕⊞🖼➡ ◈🔲♂
Photo: S. Hellner

A30832-4 *Epiplatys bifasciatus* (Steindachner, 1881)
Zweistreifen-Hechtling / Twostriped Panchax
Sierra Leone; W; 5,0 cm

▷△♬◑☺☺⊕⊞🖼➡ ◈🔲♂
Photo: L. Seegers

A30833-4 *Epiplatys bifasciatus* (Steindachner, 1881)
Zweistreifen-Hechtling / Twostriped Panchax
Bonoua, Elfenbeinküste / Ivory Coast; W; 5,0 cm

▷△♬◑☺☺⊕⊞🖼➡ ◈🔲♂
Photo: E. Pürzl

A30834-4 *Epiplatys bifasciatus* (Steindachner, 1881)
Zweistreifen-Hechtling / Twostriped Panchax
Benin; W; 5,0 cm

▷△♬◑☺☺⊕⊞🖼➡ ◈🔲♂
Photo: E. Pürzl

A30840-4 *Epiplatys boulengeri* (Pellegrin, 1926) ?
Boulengers Hechtling / Boulenger's Panchax
Lekoni Fluß, Gabun / Lekoni River, Gabon; W; 7,0 cm

△♬◑☺☺⊕⊞🖼➡ ◈🔲♂
Photo: E. Pürzl

A30841-4 *Epiplatys boulengeri* (Pellegrin, 1926) ?
Boulengers Hechtling / Boulenger's Panchax, "CHP 82/16"
Kongo / Congo; B; 7,0 cm

△♬◑☺☺⊕⊞🖼➡ ◈🔲♂
Photo: L. Seegers

A30845-4 *Epiplatys chaperi chaperi* (Sauvage, 1882)
Chapers Hechtling / Chaper's Panchax
Angona, Ghana; B; 7,0 cm

▷⚠🅱️◑☺😊🔼🖼️➡️ ◈🔲 ♂️   Photo: L. Seegers

A30846-4 *Epiplatys chaperi chaperi* (Sauvage, 1882)
Chapers Hechtling / Chaper's Panchax
Aquaristik-Import / Aquarium import, Ghana; W; 7,0 cm

▷⚠🅱️◑☺😊🔼🖼️➡️ ◈🔲 ♂️   Photo: L. Seegers

A30847-4 *Epiplatys chaperi chaperi* (Sauvage, 1882)
Chapers Hechtling / Chaper's Panchax
Awaso, Ghana; W; 7,0 cm

▷⚠🅱️◑☺😊🔼🖼️➡️ ◈🔲 ♂️   Photo: E. Pürzl

A30848-4 *Epiplatys chaperi chaperi* (Sauvage, 1882)
Chapers Hechtling / Chaper's Panchax
Ono, östlich Abidjan, Elfenbeinküste / E Abidjan, Ivory Coast; W; 7,0 cm

▷⚠🅱️◑☺😊🔼🖼️➡️ ◈🔲 ♂️   Photo: L. Seegers

A30849-4 *Epiplatys chaperi chaperi* (Sauvage, 1882)
Chapers Hechtling / Chaper's Panchax
Bonoua, Elfenbeinküste / Bonoua, Ivory Coast; W; 7,0 cm

▷⚠🅱️◑☺😊🔼🖼️➡️ ◈🔲 ♂️   Photo: E. Pürzl

A30849-4 *Epiplatys chaperi chaperi* (Sauvage, 1882)
Chapers Hechtling / Chaper's Panchax
Bonoua, Elfenbeinküste / Bonoua, Ivory Coast; W; 7,0 cm

▷⚠🅱️◑☺😊🔼🖼️➡️ ◈🔲 ♀️   Photo: E. Pürzl

A30855-4 *Epiplatys chaperi schreiberi* Berkenkamp, 1975
Schreibers Hechtling / Schreiber's Panchax, "Gh 1/74"
5 km südöstlich Kumasi, Ghana / 5 km SE Kumasi, Ghana; B; 7,0 cm

▷⚠🅱️◑☺😊🔼🖼️➡️ ◈🔲 ♂️   Photo: L. Seegers

A30855-4 *Epiplatys chaperi schreiberi* Berkenkamp, 1975
Schreibers Hechtling / Schreiber's Panchax, "Gh 1/74"
5 km südöstlich Kumasi, Ghana / 5 km SE Kumasi, Ghana; B; 7,0 cm

▷⚠🅱️◑☺😊🔼🖼️➡️ ◈🔲 ♀️   Photo: L. Seegers

A30860-4 *Epiplatys chevalieri* (Pellegrin, 1904)
Chevaliers Hechtling / Chevalier's Panchax, "RCA 91/2"
Zentralafrikanische Republik / Central African Republik; B; 6,0 cm
▷♫◑☺☺☹⬆️🖼️➡️ ⚠️ⅿ♂
Photo: H.-G. Evers

A30861-4 *Epiplatys chevalieri* (Pellegrin, 1904)
Chevaliers Hechtling / Chevalier's Panchax
Gilima, Uelé, Zaïre; B; 6,0 cm
▷♫◑☺☺☹⬆️🖼️➡️ ⚠️ⅿ♂
Photo: L. Seegers

A30862-4 *Epiplatys chevalieri* (Pellegrin, 1904)
Chevaliers Hechtling / Chevalier's Panchax
Kinshasa, Zaïre; W; 6,0 cm
▷♫◑☺☺☹⬆️🖼️➡️ ⚠️ⅿ♂
Photo: L. Seegers

A30862-4 *Epiplatys chevalieri* (Pellegrin, 1904)
Chevaliers Hechtling / Chevalier's Panchax
Kinshasa, Zaïre; W; 6,0 cm
▷♫◑☺☺☹⬆️🖼️➡️ ⚠️ⅿ♂
Photo: L. Seegers

A30863-4 *Epiplatys chevalieri* (Pellegrin, 1904)
Chevaliers Hechtling / Chevalier's Panchax, "Z 26/82"
Njili, Kinshasa, Zaïre; W; 6,0 cm
▷♫◑☺☺☹⬆️🖼️➡️ ⚠️ⅿ♂
Photo: E. Pürzl

A30863-4 *Epiplatys chevalieri* (Pellegrin, 1904)
Chevaliers Hechtling / Chevalier's Panchax, "Z 26/82"
Njili, Kinshasa, Zaïre; W; 6,0 cm
▷♫◑☺☺☹⬆️🖼️➡️ ⚠️ⅿ♀
Photo: E. Pürzl

A30864-4 *Epiplatys chevalieri* (Pellegrin, 1904)
Chevaliers Hechtling / Chevalier's Panchax
30 km SW Kinshasa, on road to Matadi, Zaïre; W; 6,0 cm
▷♫◑☺☺☹⬆️🖼️➡️ ⚠️ⅿ♂
Photo: L. Seegers

A30865-4 *Epiplatys chevalieri* (Pellegrin, 1904)
Chevaliers Hechtling / Chevalier's Panchax
Zaïre; B; 6,0 cm
▷♫◑☺☺☹⬆️🖼️➡️ ⚠️ⅿ♂
Photo: E. Schraml

A30870-4 *Epiplatys coccinatus* Berkenkamp & Etzel, 1982
Scharlach-Hechtling / Scarlet Panchax, "RL 45" (= *E. ruhkopfi* ?)
3 km N Salayea, N Liberia; W; 7,5 cm
▷ ⫤ ℙ ♬ ◑ ☺ ☺ 🎁 🖼 ➡ ◈ 🅼 ♂   Photo: L. Seegers

A30871-4 *Epiplatys coccinatus* Berkenkamp & Etzel, 1982
Scharlach-Hechtling / Scarlet Panchax, "RL 46" (= *E. ruhkopfi* ?)
3 km S Wadalna on road Gbaruka - Zorzor, central Liberia; W; 7,5 cm
▷ ⫤ ℙ ♬ ◑ ☺ ☺ 🎁 🖼 ➡ ◈ 🅼 ♂   Photo: L. Seegers

A30875-4 *Epiplatys dageti dageti* Poll, 1953
Dagets Hechtling / Daget's Panchax
N Aboisso, Elfenbeinküste / N Aboisso, Ivory Coast; W; 5,5 cm
▷ ⚠ ⫤ ℙ ♬ ◑ ☺ ☺ 🎁 🖼 ➡ ◈ 🅼 ♂   Photo: L. Seegers

A30875-4 *Epiplatys dageti dageti* Poll, 1953
Dagets Hechtling / Daget's Panchax
N Aboisso, Elfenbeinküste / N Aboisso, Ivory Coast; W; 5,5 cm
▷ ⚠ ⫤ ℙ ♬ ◑ ☺ ☺ 🎁 🖼 ➡ ◈ 🅼 ♀   Photo: L. Seegers

A30876-4 *Epiplatys dageti dageti* Poll, 1953
Dagets Hechtling / Daget's Panchax
San Pedro, Elfenbeinküste / San Pedro, Ivory Coast; W; 5,5 cm
▷ ⚠ ⫤ ℙ ♬ ◑ ☺ ☺ 🎁 🖼 ➡ ◈ 🅼 ♂   Photo: E. Pürzl

A30877-4 *Epiplatys dageti dageti* Poll, 1953
Dagets Hechtling / Daget's Panchax
Tabou, Elfenbeinküste / Tabou, Ivory Coast; W; 5,5 cm
▷ ⚠ ℙ ♬ ◑ ☺ ☺ 🎁 🖼 ➡ ◈ 🅼 ♂   Photo: E. Pürzl

A30877-3 *Epiplatys dageti dageti* Poll, 1953
Dagets Hechtling / Daget's Panchax
Tabou, Elfenbeinküste / Tabou, Ivory Coast; W; 5,5 cm
▷ ⚠ ⫤ ℙ ♬ ◑ ☺ ☺ 🎁 🖼 ➡ ◈ 🅼 ♂   Photo: L. Seegers

A30877-4 *Epiplatys dageti dageti* Poll, 1953
Dagets Hechtling / Daget's Panchax
Tabou, Elfenbeinküste / Tabou, Ivory Coast; W; 5,5 cm
▷ ⚠ ⫤ ℙ ♬ ◑ ☺ ☺ 🎁 🖼 ➡ ◈ 🅼 ♀   Photo: L. Seegers

A30878-3 *Epiplatys dageti dageti* Poll, 1953
Dagets Hechtling / Daget's Panchax
SW Ghana; W; 5,5 cm
▷△℘♫◑☺☺☹⬆️🎴➡️ ◈🔟 ♂
Photo: L. Seegers

A30878-3 *Epiplatys dageti dageti* Poll, 1953
Dagets Hechtling / Daget's Panchax
SW Ghana; W; 5,5 cm
▷△℘♫◑☺☺☹⬆️🎴➡️ ◈🔟 ♀
Photo: L. Seegers

A30885-4 *Epiplatys dageti monroviae* Daget & Arnoult, 1964
Querbandhechtling / Red Chinned Panchax
Monrovia, Liberia; W; 5,5 cm
▷△♫◑☺☺☹⬆️🎴➡️ ◈🔟 ♂
Photo: L. Seegers

A30886-4 *Epiplatys dageti monroviae* Daget & Arnoult, 1964
Querbandhechtling / Red Chinned Panchax
Aquarienstamm / Aquarium strain from Monrovia, Liberia; B; 5,5 cm
▷△♫◑☺☺☹⬆️🎴➡️ ◈🔟 ♂
Photo: L. Seegers

A30887-4 *Epiplatys dageti monroviae* Daget & Arnoult, 1964
Querbandhechtling / Red Chinned Panchax
Aquarienstamm / Aquarium strain; B; 5,5 cm
▷△♫◑☺☺☹⬆️🎴➡️ ◈🔟 ♂
Photo: H-G. Evers

A30888-4 *Epiplatys dageti monroviae* Daget & Arnoult, 1964
Querbandhechtling / Red Chinned Panchax
Xanthoristic aquarium strain; B; 5,5 cm
▷△♫◑☺☺☹⬆️🎴➡️ ◈🔟 ♀
Photo: H.-G. Evers

A30890-4 *Epiplatys esekanus* Scheel, 1968
Eseka-Hechtling / Eseka Panchax
Aquarienstamm / Aquarium strain; B; 6,5 cm
▷♫◑☺☺☹⬆️🎴➡️ △🔟 ♂
Photo: S. Hellner

A30890-4 *Epiplatys esekanus* Scheel, 1968
Eseka-Hechtling / Eseka Panchax
Aquarienstamm / Aquarium strain; B; 6,5 cm
▷♫◑☺☺☹⬆️🎴➡️ △🔟 ♀
Photo: L. Seegers

A30887-4 *Epiplatys dageti monroviae* DAGET & ARNOULT, 1964
Querbandhechtling / Red Chinned Panchax
Aquarienstamm / Aquarium strain; B; 5,5 cm

Photo: H.J. Mayland

▷△♬❶◐☺☻⊤▧➧ ◈▥ ♂

A30891-4 *Epiplatys esekanus* SCHEEL, 1968
Eseka-Hechtling / Eseka Panchax
15 Meilen nördlich Eseka nahe der Kreuzung Eseka - Yaounde - Edea, Ost-Kamerun / 15 miles north of Eseka,
near the Eseka - Yaounde - Edea junction in East Cameroon; W; 6,5 cm

Photo: E. Pürzl

▷♬❶◐☺☻⊤▧➧ ▲▥ ♂

A30890-4 *Epiplatys esekanus* SCHEEL, 1968
Eseka-Hechtling / Eseka Panchax
Aquarienstamm / Aquarium strain; B; 6,5 cm
▷♫◑☺☻⬆🐟➡ ⚠🔟 ♂
Photo: L. Seegers

A30890-4 *Epiplatys esekanus* SCHEEL, 1968
Eseka-Hechtling / Eseka Panchax
Aquarienstamm / Aquarium strain; B; 6,5 cm
▷♫◑☺☻⬆🐟➡ ⚠🔟 ♂
Photo: K. Lütje

A30895-4 *Epiplatys fasciolatus fasciolatus* (GÜNTHER, 1866)
Bänder-Hechtling / Banded Panchax
Konakry, Guinea / Conakry, Guinea; W; 9,0 cm
⚠♫◑☺☻⬆🐟➡ ◈🔟 ♂
Photo: L. Seegers

A30896-4 *Epiplatys fasciolatus fasciolatus* (GÜNTHER, 1866)
Bänder-Hechtling / Banded Panchax
Guinea; B; 9,0 cm
⚠♫◑☺☻⬆🐟➡ ◈🔟 ♂
Photo: E. Pürzl

A30897-4 *Epiplatys fasciolatus fasciolatus* (GÜNTHER, 1866)
Bänder-Hechtling / Banded Panchax
Lome, Guinea; W; 9,0 cm
⚠♫◑☺☻⬆🐟➡ ◈🔟 ♂
Photo: L. Seegers

A30896-4 *Epiplatys fasciolatus fasciolatus* (GÜNTHER, 1866)
Bänder-Hechtling / Banded Panchax
Guinea; B; 9,0 cm
⚠♫◑☺☻⬆🐟➡ ◈🔟 ♂
Photo: H.-G. Evers

A30898-4 *Epiplatys fasciolatus fasciolatus* (GÜNTHER, 1866)
Bänder-Hechtling / Banded Panchax
Bahama, Sierra Leone; W; 9,0 cm
⚠♫◑☺☻⬆🐟➡ ◈🔟 ♂
Photo: L. Seegers

A30899-4 *Epiplatys fasciolatus fasciolatus* (GÜNTHER, 1866)
Bänder-Hechtling / Banded Panchax
Bathurst, Sierra Leone; W; 9,0 cm
⚠♫◑☺☻⬆🐟➡ ◈🔟 ♂
Photo: S. Hellner

A30900-4 *Epiplatys fasciolatus fasciolatus* (Günther, 1866)
Bänder-Hechtling / Banded Panchax
Freetown, Sierra Leone; W; 9,0 cm

Photo: L. Seegers

A30900-4 *Epiplatys fasciolatus fasciolatus* (Günther, 1866)
Bänder-Hechtling / Banded Panchax
Freetown, Sierra Leone; W; 9,0 cm

Photo: L. Seegers

A30901-4 *Epiplatys fasciolatus fasciolatus* (Günther, 1866)
Bänder-Hechtling / Banded Panchax
Bo, Liberia; B; 9,0 cm

Photo: L. Seegers

A30902-4 *Epiplatys fasciolatus fasciolatus* (Günther, 1866)
Bänder-Hechtling / Banded Panchax, "RL 4"
Bo, 500 m before reaching border with Sierra Leone, Liberia; W; 9,0 cm

Photo: L. Seegers

A30903-4 *Epiplatys fasciolatus fasciolatus* (Günther, 1866)
Bänder-Hechtling / Banded Panchax, "RL 6"
200 m S Kpenigi, NW-Liberia; W; 9,0 cm

Photo: L. Seegers

A30904-4 *Epiplatys fasciolatus fasciolatus* (Günther, 1866)
Bänder-Hechtling / Banded Panchax, "RL 32"
Robertsport, Liberia; W; 9,0 cm

Photo: L. Seegers

A30905-4 *Epiplatys fasciolatus fasciolatus* (Günther, 1866)
Bänder-Hechtling / Banded Panchax, "RL 84"
500 m before Banjola, Liberia; W; 9,0 cm

Photo: L. Seegers

A30906-4 *Epiplatys fasciolatus fasciolatus* (Günther, 1866)
Bänder-Hechtling / Banded Panchax, "RL 86"
Liberia; W; 9,0 cm

Photo: L. Seegers

A30910-4 *Epiplatys fasciolatus tototaensis* ROMAND, 1978
Totota-Hechtling / Totota Panchax
Totota, Liberia; B; 9,0 cm
⚠️🐟◑☺☹🔝🖼️🐟 ◈Ⓜ️ ♂
Photo: L. Seegers

A30910-4 *Epiplatys fasciolatus tototaensis* ROMAND, 1978
Totota-Hechtling / Totota Panchax
Totota, Liberia; B; 9,0 cm
⚠️🐟◑☺☹🔝🖼️🐟 ◈Ⓜ️ ♂
Photo: L. Seegers

A30915-4 *Epiplatys fasciolatus zimiensis* BERKENKAMP, 1977
Goldener Bänder-Hechtling / Golden Banded Panchax, "SL 89"
Faimah, Sierra Leone; B; 9,0 cm
⚠️🐟◑☺☹🔝🖼️🐟 ◈Ⓜ️ ♂
Photo: E. Schraml

A30916-4 *Epiplatys fasciolatus zimiensis* BERKENKAMP, 1977
Goldener Bänder-Hechtling / Golden Banded Panchax, "SL 89"
Giemsa, Sierra Leone; W; 9,0 cm
⚠️🐟◑☺☹🔝🖼️🐟 ◈Ⓜ️ ♂
Photo: S. Hellner

A30917-4 *Epiplatys fasciolatus zimiensis* BERKENKAMP, 1977
Goldener Bänder-Hechtling / Golden Banded Panchax, "SL 89"
Rotain, Sierra Leone; B; 9,0 cm
⚠️🐟◑☺☹🔝🖼️🐟 ◈Ⓜ️ ♂
Photo: E. Schraml

A30918-4 *Epiplatys fasciolatus zimiensis* BERKENKAMP, 1977
Goldener Bänder-Hechtling / Golden Banded Panchax, "SL 89"
Perie, Sierra Leone; B; 9,0 cm
⚠️🐟◑☺☹🔝🖼️🐟 ◈Ⓜ️ ♂
Photo: E. Schraml

A30919-4 *Epiplatys fasciolatus zimiensis* BERKENKAMP, 1977
Goldener Bänder-Hechtling / Golden Banded Panchax, "SL 89"
Zimmi, Sierra Leone; W; 9,0 cm
⚠️🐟◑☺☹🔝🖼️🐟 ◈Ⓜ️ ♂
Photo: L. Seegers

A30920-4 *Epiplatys fasciolatus zimiensis* BERKENKAMP, 1977
Goldener Bänder-Hechtling / Golden Banded Panchax
Xanthoristische Mutante / Xanthoristic form; Z; 9,0 cm
⚠️🐟◑☺☹🔝🖼️🐟 ◈Ⓜ️ ♂
Photo: L. Seegers

A30925-4 *Epiplatys grahami* (BOULENGER, 1911)
Grahams Hechtling / Graham's Panchax
Gamui, Benin; F₁; 6,0 cm

Photo: L. Seegers

A30925-4 *Epiplatys grahami* (BOULENGER, 1911)
Grahams Hechtling / Graham's Panchax
Gamui, Benin; F₁; 6,0 cm

Photo: L. Seegers

A30926-4 *Epiplatys grahami* (BOULENGER, 1911)
Grahams Hechtling / Graham's Panchax
Südost Benin / Southeastern Benin; W; 6,0 cm

Photo: E. Pürzl

A30927-4 *Epiplatys grahami* (BOULENGER, 1911)
Grahams Hechtling / Graham's Panchax
Nigerdelta, Nigeria / Delta of Niger River, Nigeria; W; 6,0 cm

Photo: E. Pürzl

A30928-4 *Epiplatys grahami* (BOULENGER, 1911)
Grahams Hechtling / Graham's Panchax
Kamerun / Cameroon; B; 6,0 cm

Photo: L. Seegers

A30929-4 *Epiplatys grahami* (BOULENGER, 1911)
Grahams Hechtling / Graham's Panchax
Kribi, Kamerun / Kribi, Cameroon; W; 6,0 cm

Photo: E. Pürzl

A30930-4 *Epiplatys grahami* (BOULENGER, 1911)
Grahams Hechtling / Graham's Panchax, "HJRK 92"
Kamerun / Cameroon; W; 6,0 cm

Photo: S. Hellner

A30935-4 *Epiplatys guineensis* ROMAND, 1994
Guinea-Hechtling / Guinea Panchax
Aquarienstamm / Aquarium strain; B; 6,0 cm

Photo: H.-G. Evers

A30940-4 *Epiplatys hildegardae* Berkenkamp, 1978
Hildegards Hechtling / Hildegard's Panchax
Südost-Guinea / SE Guinea; W; 6,0 cm
▷ ♫ ◑ ☺ ☻ ⊡ ▦ ➔ ⚠ ▣ ♂

Photo: L. Seegers

A30940-4 *Epiplatys hildegardae* Berkenkamp, 1978
Hildegards Hechtling / Hildegard's Panchax
Südost-Guinea / SE Guinea; W; 6,0 cm
▷ ♫ ◑ ☺ ☻ ⊡ ▦ ➔ ⚠ ▣ ♀

Photo: L. Seegers

A30945-4 *Epiplatys huberi* Radda & Pürzl, 1981
Hubers Hechtling / Huber's Panchax
25 km ENE N'dendé on road to Lébamba, Gabon; W; 6,5 cm
◁ ▷ ♫ ◑ ☺ ☻ ⊡ ▦ ➔ ⚠ ▣ ♂

Photo: L. Seegers

A30945-4 *Epiplatys huberi* Radda & Pürzl, 1981
Hubers Hechtling / Huber's Panchax
25 km ENE N'dendé on road to Lébamba, Gabon; W; 6,5 cm
◁ ▷ ♫ ◑ ☺ ☻ ⊡ ▦ ➔ ⚠ ▣ ♀

Photo: E. Pürzl

A30950-4 *Epiplatys lamottei* Daget, 1954
Blauer Hechtling / Blue Panchax
N'Zérékoré, Guinea; B; 6,5 cm
◁ ▷ ♫ ◑ ☺ ☻ ⊡ ▦ ➔ ⚠ ▣ ♂

Photo: L. Seegers

A30950-4 *Epiplatys lamottei* Daget, 1954
Blauer Hechtling / Blue Panchax
N'Zérékoré, Guinea; B; 6,5 cm
◁ ▷ ♫ ◑ ☺ ☻ ⊡ ▦ ➔ ⚠ ▣ ♀

Photo: L. Seegers

A30950-4 *Epiplatys lamottei* Daget, 1954
Blauer Hechtling / Blue Panchax
N'Zérékoré, Guinea; B; 6,5 cm
◁ ▷ ♫ ◑ ☺ ☻ ⊡ ▦ ➔ ⚠ ▣ ♂

Photo: L. Seegers

A30950-4 *Epiplatys lamottei* Daget, 1954
Blauer Hechtling / Blue Panchax
N'Zérékoré, Guinea; B; 6,5 cm
◁ ▷ ♫ ◑ ☺ ☻ ⊡ ▦ ➔ ⚠ ▣ ♂

Photo: H.-J. Mayland

A30940-4 *Epiplatys hildegardae* Berkenkamp, 1978
Hildegards Hechtling / Hildegard's Panchax
Südóst-Guinea / SE Guinea; W; 6,0 cm

Photo: L. Seegers

A30945-4 *Epiplatys huberi* Radda & Pürzl, 1981
Hubers Hechtling / Huber's Panchax
25 km ENE N'dendé on road to Lébamba, Gabon; W; 6,5 cm

Photo: E. Pürzl

A30955-4 *Epiplatys longiventralis* (Boulenger, 1911)
Nigeria-Hechtling / Nigeria Panchax
NO von Awka, Süd-Nigeria / NE of Awka, South Nigeria; W; 6,5 cm
⚠️🔩◑☺😀🔝🖼➡️ ⚠️🔲 ♂
Photo: E. Pürzl

A30956-4 *Epiplatys longiventralis* (Boulenger, 1911)
Nigeria-Hechtling / Nigeria Panchax
Orashi River, E Nigerdelta, Süd-Nigeria / South Nigeria; W; 6,5 cm
⚠️🔩◑☺😀🔝🖼➡️ ⚠️🔲 ♂
Photo. R. Wildekamp

A30960-4 *Epiplatys mesogramma* Huber, 1980
Bangui-Hechtling / Bangui Panchax
Brook between Mbaiki and Mongoumba, S Bangui, RCA; W; 5,5 cm
▷🔩◑☺😀🔝🖼➡️ ⚠️🔲 ♂
Photo: L. Seegers

A30961-4 *Epiplatys mesogramma* Huber, 1980
Bangui-Hechtling / Bangui Panchax
Aquarienstamm / Aquarium strain; B; 5,5 cm
▷🔩◑☺😀🔝🖼➡️ ⚠️🔲 ♂
Photo: L. Seegers

A30962-4 *Epiplatys* cf. *mesogramma* Huber, 1980
Bangui-Hechtling / Bangui Panchax, "Z 86/15"
Provinz Equateur, Zaïre / Equateur province, Zaïre; W; 5,5 cm
▷🔩◑☺😀🔝🖼➡️ ⚠️🔲 ♂
Photo: L. Seegers

A30965-4 *Epiplatys* aff. *multifasciatus* (Boulenger, 1913)
Vielstreifenhechtling / Multibarred Panchax
Provinz Equateur, Zaïre / Equateur province, Zaïre; W; 5,5 cm
▷🔩◑☺😀🔝🖼➡️ ⚠️🔲 ♂
Photo: L. Seegers

A30966-4 *Epiplatys multifasciatus* (Boulenger, 1913)
Vielstreifenhechtling / Multibarred Panchax
Masekpe, Equateur province, Zaïre; W; 5,5 cm
▷🔩◑☺😀🔝🖼➡️ ⚠️🔲 ♂
Photo: L. Seegers

A30966-4 *Epiplatys multifasciatus* (Boulenger, 1913)
Vielstreifenhechtling / Multibarred Panchax
Masekpe, Equateur province, Zaïre; W; 5,5 cm
▷🔩◑☺😀🔝🖼➡️ ⚠️🔲 ♀
Photo: L. Seegers

A30966-4 *Epiplatys multifasciatus* (Boulenger, 1913)
Vielstreifenhechtling / Multibarred Panchax
Masekpe, Equateur province, Zaïre; W; 5,5 cm
▷🐟◑☺😐📲🔲➡ ⚠🔲 ♂ Photo: L. Seegers

A30967-4 *Epiplatys multifasciatus* (Boulenger, 1913)
Vielstreifenhechtling / Multibarred Panchax
Wamba-Fluß, Zaïre / Wamba River, Zaïre; W; 5,5 cm
▷🐟◑☺😐📲🔲➡ ⚠🔲 ♂ Photo: E. Pürzl

A30968-4 *Epiplatys* aff. *multifasciatus* (Boulenger, 1913)
Vielstreifenhechtling / Multibarred Panchax
26 km from Kananga on road to Mbuji Mayi, Zaïre; W; 5,5 cm
▷🐟◑☺😐📲🔲➡ ⚠🔲 ♂ Photo: L. Seegers

A30970-4 *Epiplatys njalaensis* Neumann, 1976
Njalahechtling / Njala Panchax, "SL 89"
Hojieh River, Sierra Leone; W; 5,5 cm
⚠🐟◑☺😐📲🔲➡ ⚠🔲 ♂ Photo: S. Hellner

A30971-4 *Epiplatys njalaensis* Neumann, 1976
Njalahechtling / Njala Panchax
Rinka River at Munguna, Sierra Leone; W; 5,5 cm
⚠🐟◑☺😐📲🔲➡ ⚠🔲 ♂ Photo: E. Pürzl

A30972-4 *Epiplatys njalaensis* Neumann, 1976
Njalahechtling / Njala Panchax
NW Liberia; W; 5,5 cm
⚠🐟◑☺😐📲🔲➡ ⚠🔲 ♂ Photo: L. Seegers

A30973-4 *Epiplatys njalaensis* Neumann, 1976
Njalahechtling / Njala Panchax
Kenema, Sierra Leone; W; 5,5 cm
⚠🐟◑☺😐📲🔲➡ ⚠🔲 ♂ Photo: L. Seegers

A30973-4 *Epiplatys njalaensis* Neumann, 1976
Njalahechtling / Njala Panchax
Kenema, Sierra Leone; W; 5,5 cm
⚠🐟◑☺😐📲🔲➡ ⚠🔲 ♀ Photo: L. Seegers

A30975-4 *Epiplatys olbrechtsi* POLL, 1941
Olbrechts Hechtling / Olbrecht's Panchax
Südöstliche Elfenbeinküste / SE Ivory Coast; W; 8,5 cm

Photo: L. Seegers

A30976-4 *Epiplatys olbrechtsi* POLL, 1941
Olbrechts Hechtling / Olbrecht's Panchax
Grenze Liberia-Elfenbeinküste / Border Liberia-Ivory Coast; W; 8,5 cm

Photo: L. Seegers

A30977-4 *Epiplatys olbrechtsi* POLL, 1941
Olbrechts Hechtling / Olbrecht's Panchax, "RL 52"
Liberia; W; 8,5 cm

Photo: L. Seegers

A30978-4 *Epiplatys olbrechtsi* POLL, 1941
Olbrechts Hechtling / Olbrecht's Panchax, "RL 79"
2 km nach Suehn, Liberia / 2 km after Suehn, Liberia; W; 8,5 cm

Photo: L. Seegers

A30979-4 *Epiplatys olbrechtsi* POLL, 1941
Olbrechts Hechtling / Olbrecht's Panchax, "RL 82"
3 miles S of entrance of LAC-plantation, Modebi, Liberia; W; 8,5 cm

Photo: L. Seegers

A30980-4 *Epiplatys olbrechtsi* POLL, 1941
Olbrechts Hechtling / Olbrecht's Panchax
Grand Bereby, Elfenbeinküste / Ivory Coast; W; 8,5 cm

Photo: E. Pürzl

A30981-4 *Epiplatys olbrechtsi* POLL, 1941
Olbrechts Hechtling / Olbrecht's Panchax, "CI 43"
Kassiapleu, Elfenbeinküste / Ivory Coast; W; 8,5 cm

Photo: L. Seegers

A30982-4 *Epiplatys olbrechtsi* POLL, 1941
Olbrechts Hechtling / Olbrecht's Panchax, "RL 56"
Yreah, Liberia; W; 8,5 cm (= *E. azureus* BERKENKAMP & ETZEL, 1983)

Photo: L. Seegers

A30983-4 *Epiplatys olbrechtsi* POLL, 1941 (= *E. fasciolatus puetzi* BERKENKAMP & ETZEL, 1985)   Photo: L. Seegers
Olbrechts Hechtling / Olbrecht's Panchax, "RL 86"
20 km N Buchanan, Liberia; B; 8,5 cm

A30986-4 *Epiplatys roloffi* ROMAND, 1978   Photo: L. Seegers
Roloffs Hechtling / Roloff's Panchax
Salayea, Nord-Liberia / Northern Liberia; B; 8,0 cm

A30985-4 *Epiplatys roloffi* ROMAND, 1978
Roloffs Hechtling / Roloff's Panchax, "RL 99"
12 miles from Voinjama to Kolahun, Liberia; B; 8,0 cm
Photo: H.-G. Evers

A30986-4 *Epiplatys roloffi* ROMAND, 1978
Roloffs Hechtling / Roloff's Panchax
Salayea, Nord-Liberia / Northern Liberia; B; 8,0 cm
Photo: L. Seegers

A30990-4 *Epiplatys ruhkopfi* BERKENKAMP & ETZEL, 1980
Ruhkopfs Hechtling / Ruhkopf's Panchax
Salayea, Nord-Liberia / Salayea, Northern Liberia; B; 8,0 cm
Photo: L. Seegers

A30995-4 *Epiplatys sangmelinensis neumanni* (BERKENKAMP, 1993)
Neumanns Sangmelima-Hechtling / Neumann's Sangmelima Panchax
Akono, Kamerun / Akono, Cameroon; W; 6,5 cm [valid subspecies ?]
Photo: L. Seegers

A30997-4 *Epiplatys sangmelinensis sangmelinensis* (AHL, 1928)
Sangmelima-Hechtling / Sangmelima Panchax
Mbalmayo, Kamerun / Mbalmayo, Cameroon; W; 6,5 cm
Photo: E. Pürzl

A30996-4 *Epiplatys sangmelinensis neumanni* (BERKENKAMP, 1993)
Neumanns Sangmelima-Hechtling / Neumann's Sangmelima Panchax
Akonotangam, Kamerun / Akonotangam, Cameroon; W; 6,5 cm
Photo: R. Wildekamp

A30998-4 *Epiplatys sangmelinensis sangmelinensis* (AHL, 1928)
Sangmelima-Hechtling / Sangmelima Panchax
Umgebung von Sangmelima / Sangmelima area, Cameroon; W; 6,5 cm
Photo: L. Seegers

A30999-4 *Epiplatys sangmelinensis sangmelinensis* (AHL, 1928)
Sangmelima-Hechtling / Sangmelima Panchax
Ovan, Gabun / Ovan, Gabon; W; 6,5 cm
Photo: E. Pürzl

A30700-4 *Epiplatys sexfasciatus togolensis* Loiselle, 1971
Togohechtling / Togo Panchax
Palime, Togo; W; 8,0 cm

▷🎣◐☺☻⬆🏞🐾 ◈m♂　　　Photo: E. Pürzl

A30701-4 *Epiplatys sexfasciatus togolensis* Loiselle, 1971
Togohechtling / Togo Panchax
SO Palime, Togo / SE Palime, Togo; W; 8,0 cm

▷🎣◐☺☻⬆🏞🐾 ◈m♂　　　Photo: E. Pürzl

A30702-4 *Epiplatys sexfasciatus togolensis* Loiselle, 1971
Togohechtling / Togo Panchax
Togo; B; 8,0 cm

▷🎣◐☺☻⬆🏞🐾 ◈m♂　　　Photo: L. Seegers

A30702-4 *Epiplatys sexfasciatus togolensis* Loiselle, 1971
Togohechtling / Togo Panchax
Togo; B; 8,0 cm

▷🎣◐☺☻⬆🏞🐾 ◈m♀　　　Photo: L. Seegers

A30703-4 *Epiplatys sexfasciatus togolensis* Loiselle, 1971
Togohechtling / Togo Panchax, "RT 18"
Togo; B; 8,0 cm

▷🎣◐☺☻⬆🏞🐾 ◈m♂　　　Photo: R. Lütje

A30704-4 *Epiplatys sexfasciatus togolensis* Loiselle, 1971
Togohechtling / Togo Panchax
Djigbe, Benin; B; 8,0 cm

▷🎣◐☺☻⬆🏞🐾 ◈m♂　　　Photo: E. Pürzl

A30705-4 *Epiplatys sexfasciatus togolensis* Loiselle, 1971
Togohechtling / Togo Panchax
Igolo, Benin; F1; 8,0 cm

▷🎣◐☺☻⬆🏞🐾 ◈m♂　　　Photo: L. Seegers

A30706-4 *Epiplatys sexfasciatus togolensis* Loiselle, 1971
Togohechtling / Togo Panchax
Benin; W; 8,0 cm

▷🎣◐☺☻⬆🏞🐾 ◈m♂　　　Photo: E. Pürzl

A30710-4 *Epiplatys sexfasciatus infrafasciatus* (Günther, 1866)
Calabarhechtling / Calabar Panchax
Nigeria; B; 8,0 cm
▷♬❍☺☹⬆🖼🐟 ◈🖼♂
Photo: L. Seegers

A30711-4 *Epiplatys sexfasciatus infrafasciatus* (Günther, 1866)
Calabarhechtling / Calabar Panchax
Taylor Creek, Nigeria; B; 8,0 cm
▷♬❍☺☹⬆🖼🐟 ◈🖼♂
Photo: E. Pürzl

A30712-4 *Epiplatys sexfasciatus infrafasciatus* (Günther, 1866)
Calabarhechtling / Calabar Panchax, "HJRK 92"
Kamerun / Cameroon; B; 8,0 cm
▷♬❍☺☹⬆🖼🐟 ◈🖼♂
Photo: S. Hellner

A30713-4 *Epiplatys sexfasciatus infrafasciatus* (Günther, 1866)
Calabarhechtling / Calabar Panchax
Tinto, Kamerun / Tinto, Cameroon; B; 8,0 cm
▷♬❍☺☹⬆🖼🐟 ◈🖼♂
Photo: E. Pürzl

A30715-4 *Epiplatys sexfasciatus rathkei* Radda, 1971
Kumbahechtling / Kumba Panchax
Kumba, Kamerun / Kumba, Cameroon; W; 8,0 cm
▷♬❍☺☹⬆🖼🐟 ◈🖼♂
Photo: E. Pürzl

A30715-4 *Epiplatys sexfasciatus rathkei* Radda, 1971
Kumbahechtling / Kumba Panchax
Kumba, Kamerun / Kumba, Cameroon; W; 8,0 cm
▷♬❍☺☹⬆🖼🐟 ◈🖼♂
Photo: L. Seegers

A30715-4 *Epiplatys sexfasciatus rathkei* Radda, 1971
Kumbahechtling / Kumba Panchax
Kumba, Kamerun / Kumba, Cameroon; W; 8,0 cm
▷♬❍☺☹⬆🖼🐟 ◈🖼♂
Photo: L. Seegers

A30715-4 *Epiplatys sexfasciatus rathkei* Radda, 1971
Kumbahechtling / Kumba Panchax
Kumba, Kamerun / Kumba, Cameroon; W; 8,0 cm
▷♬❍☺☹⬆🖼🐟 ◈🖼♀
Photo: L. Seegers

A30716-4 *Epiplatys sexfasciatus rathkei* RADDA, 1971
Kumbahechtling / Kumba Panchax
Barombi-See, Kamerun / Lake Barombi Mbo, Cameroon; W; 8,0 cm

Photo: L. Seegers

▷🦐◑☺☹⬆🖼🐟 ◈🔲♂

A30728-4 *Epiplatys sexfasciatus baroi* BERKENKAMP, 1975
Baros Hechtling / Baro's Panchax
Makondou, Kamerun / Makondou, Cameroon; B; 8,0 cm

Photo: E. Pürzl

▷🦐◑☺☹⬆🖼🐟 ◈🔲♂

A30717-4 *Epiplatys sexfasciatus rathkei* RADDA, 1971
Kumbahechtling / Kumba Panchax
23 km from Mamfe on road to Ejoumojok, Cameroon; W; 8,0 cm

▷ ♬ ◑ ☺ ☺ ⊡ ⊡ ➡ ◈ ⊞ ♂

Photo: L. Seegers

A30718-4 *Epiplatys sexfasciatus rathkei* RADDA, 1971
Kumbahechtling / Kumba Panchax
Somakak, Kamerun / Somakak, Cameroon; W; 8,0 cm

▷ ♬ ◑ ☺ ☺ ⊡ ⊡ ➡ ◈ ⊞ ♂

Photo: E. Pürzl

A30719-4 *Epiplatys sexfasciatus rathkei* RADDA, 1971
Kumbahechtling / Kumba Panchax
Westlich Eseka, Kamerun / West of Eseka, Cameroon; W; 8,0 cm

▷ ♬ ◑ ☺ ☺ ⊡ ⊡ ➡ ◈ ⊞ ♂

Photo: E. Pürzl

A30720-4 *Epiplatys sexfasciatus rathkei* RADDA, 1971
Kumbahechtling / Kumba Panchax
Malawe, Kamerun / Malawe, Cameroon; W; 8,0 cm

▷ ♬ ◑ ☺ ☺ ⊡ ⊡ ➡ ◈ ⊞ ♂

Photo: L. Seegers

A30720-4 *Epiplatys sexfasciatus rathkei* RADDA, 1971
Kumbahechtling / Kumba Panchax
Malawe, Kamerun / Malawe, Cameroon; W; 8,0 cm

▷ ♬ ◑ ☺ ☺ ⊡ ⊡ ➡ ◈ ⊞ ♀

Photo: L. Seegers

A30725-4 *Epiplatys sexfasciatus baroi* Berkenkamp, 1975
Baros Hechtling / Baro's Panchax
Campo, Süd-Kamerun / Campo, southern Cameroon; W; 8,0 cm
Photo: L. Seegers

A30726-4 *Epiplatys sexfasciatus baroi* Berkenkamp, 1975
Baros Hechtling / Baro's Panchax
Song Dong, Kamerun / Song Dong, Cameroon; B; 8,0 cm
Photo: E. Schraml

A30727-4 *Epiplatys sexfasciatus baroi* Berkenkamp, 1975
Baros Hechtling / Baro's Panchax
Aquarienstamm, Kamerun / Aquarium strain, Cameroon; B; 8,0 cm
Photo: L. Seegers

A30727-4 *Epiplatys sexfasciatus baroi* Berkenkamp, 1975
Baros Hechtling / Baro's Panchax
Aquarienstamm, Kamerun / Aquarium strain, Cameroon; B; 8,0 cm
Photo: L. Seegers

A30728-4 *Epiplatys sexfasciatus baroi* Berkenkamp, 1975
Baros Hechtling / Baro's Panchax
Makondou, Kamerun / Makondou, Cameroon; B; 8,0 cm
Photo: L. Seegers

A30729-4 *Epiplatys sexfasciatus baroi* Berkenkamp, 1975
Baros Hechtling / Baro's Panchax
Südlich Edea, Kamerun / South of Edea, Cameroon; W; 8,0 cm
Photo: E. Pürzl

A30735-4 *Epiplatys sexfasciatus sexfasciatus* Gill, 1862
Sechsbandhechtling / Six Barred Panchax
Cocobeach, Gabun / Cocobeach, Gabon; W; 8,0 cm
Photo: E. Pürzl

A30735-4 *Epiplatys sexfasciatus sexfasciatus* Gill, 1862
Sechsbandhechtling / Six Barred Panchax
Cocobeach, Gabun / Cocobeach, Gabon; W; 8,0 cm
Photo: E. Pürzl

A30770-4 *Epiplatys sheljuzhkoi* POLL, 1953
Sheljuzhkos Hechtling / Sheljuzhko's Panchax
Aquarienstamm von Ghana / Aquarium strain from Ghana; B; 7,0 cm
▷△🛡️◑☺☹🎴🖼️🐛 ◈🖩 ♂ Photo: L. Seegers

A30771-4 *Epiplatys sheljuzhkoi* POLL, 1953
Sheljuzhkos Hechtling / Sheljuzhko's Panchax
Elfenbeinküste / Ivory Coast; W; 7,0 cm
▷△🛡️◑☺☹🎴🖼️🐛 ◈🖩 ♂ Photo: E. Pürzl

A30772-4 *Epiplatys sheljuzhkoi* POLL, 1953
Sheljuzhkos Hechtling / Sheljuzhko's Panchax
Bonoua, Elfenbeinküste / Bonoua, Ivory Coast; W; 7,0 cm
▷△🛡️◑☺☹🎴🖼️🐛 ◈🖩 ♂ Photo: E. Pürzl

A30772-4 *Epiplatys sheljuzhkoi* POLL, 1953
Sheljuzhkos Hechtling / Sheljuzhko's Panchax
Bonoua, Elfenbeinküste / Bonoua, Ivory Coast; W; 7,0 cm
▷△🛡️◑☺☹🎴🖼️🐛 ◈🖩 ♀ Photo: E. Pürzl

A30772-4 *Epiplatys sheljuzhkoi* POLL, 1953
Sheljuzhkos Hechtling / Sheljuzhko's Panchax
Bonoua, Elfenbeinküste / Bonoua, Ivory Coast; B; 7,0 cm
▷△🛡️◑☺☹🎴🖼️🐛 ◈🖩 ♂ Photo: L. Seegers

A30771-4 *Epiplatys sheljuzhkoi* POLL, 1953
Sheljuzhkos Hechtling / Sheljuzhko's Panchax
Elfenbeinküste / Ivory Coast; W; 7,0 cm
▷△🛡️◑☺☹🎴🖼️🐛 ◈🖩 ♂ Photo: E. Pürzl

A30773-4 *Epiplatys sheljuzhkoi* POLL, 1953
Sheljuzhkos Hechtling / Sheljuzhko's Panchax
Togo; W; 7,0 cm
▷△🛡️◑☺☹🎴🖼️🐛 ◈🖩 ♂ Photo: E. Pürzl

A30774-4 *Epiplatys sheljuzhkoi* POLL, 1953
Sheljuzhkos Hechtling / Sheljuzhko's Panchax
Aquarienstamm / Aquarium strain; B; 7,0 cm
▷△🛡️◑☺☹🎴🖼️🐛 ◈🖩 ♂ Photo: H.-G. Evers

A30780-4 *Epiplatys singa* (Boulenger, 1899)
Punktierter Hechtling / Spotted Panchax, "G 92/1"
Gabun / Gabon; B; 6,0 cm
▷ ♫ ◑ ☺ ☻ ⊕ ▧ ➤ ◈ ▥ ♂   Photo: H.-G. Evers

A30781-4 *Epiplatys singa* (Boulenger, 1899)
Punktierter Hechtling / Spotted Panchax, "GBN 88/8"
Gabun / Gabon; B; 6,0 cm
▷ ♫ ◑ ☺ ☻ ⊕ ▧ ➤ ◈ ▥ ♂   Photo: E. Schraml

A30780-4 *Epiplatys singa* (Boulenger, 1899)
Punktierter Hechtling / Spotted Panchax, "G 92/1"
Gabun / Gabon; B; 6,0 cm
▷ ♫ ◑ ☺ ☻ ⊕ ▧ ➤ ◈ ▥ ♂   Photo: L. Seegers

A30782-4 *Epiplatys singa* (Boulenger, 1899)
Punktierter Hechtling / Spotted Panchax
Boma, Zaïre; B; 6,0 cm
▷ ♫ ◑ ☺ ☻ ⊕ ▧ ➤ ◈ ▥ ♂   Photo: L. Seegers

A30783-4 *Epiplatys singa* (Boulenger, 1899)
Punktierter Hechtling / Spotted Panchax
Mayumba, Gabun / Mayumba, Gabon; W; 6,0 cm
▷ ♫ ◑ ☺ ☻ ⊕ ▧ ➤ ◈ ▥ ♂   Photo: E. Pürzl

A30782-4 *Epiplatys singa* (Boulenger, 1899)
Punktierter Hechtling / Spotted Panchax
Boma, Zaïre; B; 6,0 cm
▷ ♫ ◑ ☺ ☻ ⊕ ▧ ➤ ◈ ▥ ♂   Photo: E. Pürzl

A30784-4 *Epiplatys singa* (Boulenger, 1899)
Punktierter Hechtling / Spotted Panchax
Moanda, Zaïre; W; 6,0 cm
▷ ♫ ◑ ☺ ☻ ⊕ ▧ ➤ ◈ ▥ ♂   Photo: E. Pürzl

A30784-4 *Epiplatys singa* (Boulenger, 1899)
Punktierter Hechtling / Spotted Panchax
Moanda, Zaïre; W; 6,0 cm
▷ ♫ ◑ ☺ ☻ ⊕ ▧ ➤ ◈ ▥ ♀   Photo: E. Pürzl

A30790-4 *Epiplatys spilargyreius* (DUMÉRIL, 1861)
Schrägbandhechtling / Oblique Barred Panchax
Abuko, Gambia; W; 6,0 cm
▷△♗◑❶☺☻⬚🖼➡ ⚠ⓜ♂
Photo: L. Seegers

A30790-4 *Epiplatys spilargyreius* (DUMÉRIL, 1861)
Schrägbandhechtling / Oblique Barred Panchax
Abuko, Gambia; W; 6,0 cm
▷△♗◑❶☺☻⬚🖼➡ ⚠ⓜ♂
Photo: L. Seegers

A30791-3 *Epiplatys spilargyreius* (DUMÉRIL, 1861)
Schrägbandhechtling / Oblique Barred Panchax, "GAM 95/2"
Kampant, Gambia; B; 6,0 cm
▷△♗◑☺☻⬚🖼➡ ⚠ⓜ♂
Photo: H.-G. Evers

A30792-4 *Epiplatys spilargyreius* (DUMÉRIL, 1861)
Schrägbandhechtling / Oblique Barred Panchax
Kitki, Gambia; B; 6,0 cm
▷△♗❶☺☻⬚🖼➡ ⚠ⓜ♂
Photo: E. Schraml

A30793-4 *Epiplatys spilargyreius* (DUMÉRIL, 1861)
Schrägbandhechtling / Oblique Barred Panchax
Casamance, Senegal; W; 6,0 cm
▷△♗❶☺☻⬚🖼➡ ⚠ⓜ♂
Photo: L. Seegers

A30794-4 *Epiplatys spilargyreius* (DUMÉRIL, 1861)
Schrägbandhechtling / Oblique Barred Panchax
Foul Ndank, Guinea; B; 6,0 cm
▷△♗❶☺☻⬚🖼➡ ⚠ⓜ♂
Photo: L. Seegers

A30795-4 *Epiplatys spilargyreius* (DUMÉRIL, 1861)
Schrägbandhechtling / Oblique Barred Panchax
Pool Malebo, Zaïre; W; 6,0 cm
▷△♗◑☺☻⬚🖼➡ ⚠ⓜ♂
Photo: E. Pürzl

A30795-4 *Epiplatys spilargyreius* (DUMÉRIL, 1861)
Schrägbandhechtling / Oblique Barred Panchax
Pool Malebo, Zaïre; W; 6,0 cm
▷△♗◑☺☻⬚🖼➡ ⚠ⓜ♀
Photo: E. Pürzl

A30798-4 *Epiplatys* spec.
Kufina-Hechtling / Kufina Panchax
Guinea; W; 8,0 cm

Photo: L. Seegers

A30798-4 *Epiplatys* spec.
Kufina-Hechtling / Kufina Panchax
Guinea; W; 8,0 cm

Photo: L. Seegers

A30799-3 *Epiplatys* spec.
Fwa-Hechtling / Lake Fwa Panchax
Lake Fwa, Zaïre; W; 6,0 cm

Photo: L. Seegers

A30799-4 *Epiplatys* spec.
Fwa-Hechtling / Lake Fwa Panchax
Lake Fwa, Zaïre; W; 6,0 cm

Photo: L. Seegers

A30799-4 *Epiplatys* spec.
Fwa-Hechtling / Lake Fwa Panchax
Lake Fwa, Zaïre; W; 6,0 cm

Photo: L. Seegers

A30866-4 *Epiplatys* sp. aff. *chevalieri*
Roter Hechtling / Red Panchax
30 km SW Kinshasa, Zaïre; W; 6,0 cm

Photo: L. Seegers

A30867-4 *Epiplatys* sp. aff. *chevalieri*
Roter Hechtling / Red Panchax, "GKCAR 90/5"
Malanga, Zentralafr. Republ. / Central African Republic; B; 6,0 cm

Photo: E. Schraml

A30867-4 *Epiplatys* sp. aff. *chevalieri*
Roter Hechtling / Red Panchax, "GKCAR 90/5"
Malanga, Zentralafr. Republ. / Central African Republic; B; 6,0 cm

Photo: E. Pürzl

A31150-4 *Episemion callipteron* RADDA & PÜRZL, 1987
Schönflossenhechtling / Callipteron Dwarf Panchax, "G 86/20"
6 km SE Bibasse between Oyem and Mitzic, Gabon; B; 4,0 cm
▷ ⚡ ◑ ☺ ☹ ⊞ 🐟➤ ⚠ Ⓢ ♂   Photo: L. Seegers

A31150-4 *Episemion callipteron* RADDA & PÜRZL, 1987
Schönflossenhechtling / Callipteron Dwarf Panchax, "G 86/20"
6 km SE Bibasse between Oyem and Mitzic, Gabon; B; 4,0 cm
▷ ⚡ ◑ ☺ ☹ ⊞ 🐟➤ ⚠ Ⓢ ♀   Photo: L. Seegers

A31150-4 *Episemion callipteron* RADDA & PÜRZL, 1987
Schönflossenhechtling / Callipteron Dwarf Panchax, "G 86/20"
6 km SE Bibasse between Oyem and Mitzic, Gabon; B; 4,0 cm
▷ ⚡ ◑ ☺ ☹ ⊞ 🐟➤ ⚠ Ⓢ ♂   Photo: R. Lütje

A31150-4 *Episemion callipteron* RADDA & PÜRZL, 1987
Schönflossenhechtling / Callipteron Dwarf Panchax, "G 86/20"
6 km SE Bibasse between Oyem and Mitzic, Gabon; W; 4,0 cm
▷ ⚡ ◑ ☺ ☹ ⊞ 🐟➤ ⚠ Ⓢ ♂   Photo: E. Pürzl

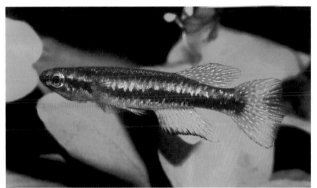

A31151-4 *Episemion callipteron* RADDA & PÜRZL, 1987
Schönflossenhechtling / Callipteron Dwarf Panchax, "GEB 94/25"
Gabun / Gabon; B; 4,0 cm
▷ ⚡ ◑ ☺ ☹ ⊞ 🐟➤ ⚠ Ⓢ ♂   Photo: R. Lütje

A31152-4 *Episemion callipteron* RADDA & PÜRZL, 1987
Schönflossenhechtling / Callipteron Dwarf Panchax
Gabun / Gabon; B; 4,0 cm
▷ ⚡ ◑ ☺ ☹ ⊞ 🐟➤ ⚠ Ⓢ ♂   Photo: H.-G. Evers

A31900-4 *Foerschichthys flavipinnis* (MEINKEN, 1932)
Gelbflossenleuchtauge / Yellow Finned Lampeye
Süd-Benin / Southern Benin; W; 3,0 cm
⚠ ⚡ ◑ ☺ 🔲 🐟➤ ⚠ Ⓢ Ⓢ ♂   Photo: E. Pürzl

A31901-4 *Foerschichthys flavipinnis* (MEINKEN, 1932)
Gelbflossenleuchtauge / Yellow Finned Lampeye
Aquarienstamm, S Nigeria / Aquarium strain, S Nigeria; B; 3,0 cm
⚠ ⚡ ◑ ☺ 🔲 🐟➤ ⚠ Ⓢ Ⓢ ♀   Photo: L. Seegers

A31955-4 *Fundulosoma thierryi* AHL, 1924
Togo-Prachtkärpfling / Togo Killifish, "RT 6/85"
Atekope, Togo; B; 3,0 cm

Photo: L. Seegers

⚠🐌◐☺☹⬇🐟🦐 ⚠Ⓢ♂

A31956-4 *Fundulosoma thierryi* AHL, 1924
Togo-Prachtkärpfling / Togo Killifish
SO Ghana, "Kluges Stamm" / SE Ghana, "Kluge's strain"; B; 3,0 cm

⚠🐌◐☺☹⬇🐟🦐 ⚠Ⓢ♂

Photo: L. Seegers

A31955-4 *Fundulosoma thierryi* AHL, 1924
Togo-Prachtkärpfling / Togo Killifish, "RT 6/85"
Atekope, Togo; B; 3,0 cm

Photo: L. Seegers

⚠🐌◐☺☹⬇🐟🦐 ⚠Ⓢ♀

A31957-3 *Fundulosoma thierryi* AHL, 1924
Togo-Prachtkärpfling / Togo Killifish
Mali; B; 3,0 cm

⚠🐌◐☺☹⬇🐟🦐 ⚠Ⓢ♂

Photo: L. Seegers

A31958-4 *Fundulosoma thierryi* AHL, 1924
Togo-Prachtkärpfling / Togo Killifish, "Gh 1/94"
Accra Plains, Ghana; B; 3,0 cm

⚠🐌◐☺☹⬇🐟🦐 ⚠Ⓢ♂

Photo: R. Wildekamp

Photo: L. Seegers

Photo: L. Seegers

Photo: L. Seegers

1 Biotop von *Nothobranchius neumanni* im Lake Manyara-Einzug, Tansania, in der Regenzeit.
2 Der gleiche Tümpel in der Trockenzeit.
3 *Nothobranchius neumanni*, der in diesem Tümpel zu findende Saisonfisch.

1 Biotop of *Nothobranchius neumanni* in the Lake Manyara drainage, Tanzania, in the rainy season.
2 The same pool in the dry season.
3 *Nothobranchius neumanni*, the seasonal fish which can be collected here.

A50000-4 *Nothobranchius bojiensis* WILDEKAMP & HAAS, 1992
Boji-Prachtgrundkärpfling / Boji Nothobranch [Holotype]
Boji-Ebene, N Merti, Kenia / Boji Plains, N Merti, Kenya; W; 6,0 cm
⚠ 🐟 🏵 ◑ ☺ 😁 ⬇ 🏞 🐾 ⚠ Ⓢ ♂
Photo: L. Seegers

A50010-4 *Nothobranchius eggersi* SEEGERS, 1982
Orchideen-Prachtgrundkärpfling / Orchid Nothobranch, Form blue
Ruhoi-Fluß, Ost-Tanzania / Ruhoi River, Eastern Tanzania; F1; 4,5 cm
⚠ 🐟 ◑ ☺ 😁 ⬇ 🏞 🐾 ⚠ Ⓢ ♂
Photo: L. Seegers

A50010-4 *Nothobranchius eggersi* SEEGERS, 1982
Orchideen-Prachtgrundkärpfling / Orchid Nothobranch, Form blue
Ruhoi-Fluß, Ost-Tanzania / Ruhoi River, Eastern Tanzania; W; 4,5 cm
⚠ 🐟 ◑ ☺ 😁 ⬇ 🏞 🐾 ⚠ Ⓢ ♂
Photo: L. Seegers

A50010-4 *Nothobranchius eggersi* SEEGERS, 1982
Orchideen-Prachtgrundkärpfling / Orchid Nothobranch, Form blue
Ruhoi-Fluß, Ost-Tanzania / Ruhoi River, Eastern Tanzania; W; 4,5 cm
⚠ 🐟 ◑ ☺ 😁 ⬇ 🏞 🐾 ⚠ Ⓢ ♀
Photo: L. Seegers

A50011-4 *Nothobranchius eggersi* SEEGERS, 1982
Orchideen-Prachtgrundkärpfling / Orchid Nothobranch, Form "red"
Rufiji River Camp, Selous Game Reserve, Eastern Tanzania; W; 4,5 cm
⚠ 🐟 ◑ ☺ 😁 ⬇ 🏞 🐾 ⚠ Ⓢ ♂
Photo: L. Seegers

A50010-4 *Nothobranchius eggersi* SEEGERS, 1982
Orchideen-Prachtgrundkärpfling / Orchid Nothobranch, Form blue
Ruhoi-Fluß, Ost-Tanzania / Ruhoi River, Eastern Tanzania; F1; 4,5 cm
⚠ 🐟 ◑ ☺ 😁 ⬇ 🏞 🐾 ⚠ Ⓢ ♂
Photo: L. Seegers

A50012-4 *Nothobranchius eggersi* SEEGERS, 1982, Form "gold"
Orchideen-Prachtgrundkärpfling / Orchid Nothobranch, "TZ 97/55"
20 km SW Utete, Rufiji drainage, Eastern Tanzania; W; 4,5 cm
⚠ 🐟 ◑ ☺ 😁 ⬇ 🏞 🐾 ⚠ Ⓢ ♂
Photo: L. Seegers

A50013-4 *Nothobranchius eggersi* SEEGERS, 1982
Orchideen-Prachtgrundkärpfling / Orchid Nothobranch, "TZ 97/4"
Kanga, Ruvu drainage, Eastern Tanzania; W; 4,5 cm
⚠ 🐟 ◑ ☺ 😁 ⬇ 🏞 🐾 ⚠ Ⓢ ♂
Photo: L. Seegers

A50020-4 *Nothobranchius elongatus* WILDEKAMP, 1982
Gestreckter Prachtgrundkärpfling / Elongate Nothobranch
Kombeni drainage north of Mombasa, Kenya; W; 5,0 cm
⚠️🦐🌓☺️😁⬇️🖼️➽ ⚠️🆂♂️   Photo: L. Seegers

A50021-4 *Nothobranchius elongatus* WILDEKAMP, 1982
Gestreckter Prachtgrundkärpfling / Elongate Nothobranch
Aquarienstamm / Aquarium strain; W; 5,0 cm
⚠️🦐🌓☺️😁⬇️🖼️➽ ⚠️🆂♂️   Photo: L. Seegers

A50027-4 *Nothobranchius fasciatus* WILDEKAMP & HAAS, 1992
Gebänderter Prachtgrundkärpfling / Barred Nothobranch
Goba B, Somalia; W; 6,0 cm
⚠️🦐🌓☺️😁⬇️🖼️➽ ⚠️🆂♂️   Photo: L. Seegers

A50027-4 *Nothobranchius fasciatus* WILDEKAMP & HAAS, 1992
Gebänderter Prachtgrundkärpfling / Barred Nothobranch
Goba B, Somalia; W; 6,0 cm
⚠️🦐🌓☺️😁⬇️🖼️➽ ⚠️🆂♀️   Photo: L. Seegers

A50030-4 *Nothobranchius foerschi* WILDEKAMP & BERKENKAMP, 1979
Foerschs Prachtgrundkärpfling /Foersch's Nothobranch
Aquarium strain, reportedly from Soga, Eastern Tanzania; B; 4,5 cm
⚠️🦐🌓☺️😁⬇️🖼️➽ ◈🆂♂️   Photo: L. Seegers

A50031-4 *Nothobranchius foerschi* WILDEKAMP & BERKENKAMP, 1979
Foerschs Prachtgrundkärpfling /Foersch's Nothobranch, "TZ 95/18"
5 km SW Kibaha on road to Soga, Tanzania; W; 4,5 cm
⚠️🦐🌓☺️😁⬇️🖼️➽ ◈🆂♂️   Photo: L. Seegers

A50032-4 *Nothobranchius foerschi* WILDEKAMP & BERKENKAMP, 1979
Foerschs Prachtgrundkärpfling /Foersch's Nothobranch, "TZ 91/103"
Ruvu plain W of Bagamoyo, Eastern Tanzania; W; 4,5 cm
⚠️🦐🌓☺️😁⬇️🖼️➽ ◈🆂♂️   Photo: L. Seegers

A50032-4 *Nothobranchius foerschi* WILDEKAMP & BERKENKAMP, 1979
Foerschs Prachtgrundkärpfling /Foersch's Nothobranch, "TZ 92/104"
Ruvu plain W Bagamoyo, Eastern Tanzania; W; 4,5 cm
⚠️🦐🌓☺️😁⬇️🖼️➽ ◈🆂♂️   Photo: L. Seegers

A50040-4 *Nothobranchius furzeri* Jubb, 1971
Furzers Prachtgrundkärpfling / Furzer's Nothobranch
Ghona re Zou Game Reserve, Zimbabwe; B; 6,5 cm

▷♬◑☺☻⊡▨➠ ⚠⑤♂   _{Photo: L. Seegers}

A50040-4 *Nothobranchius furzeri* Jubb, 1971
Furzers Prachtgrundkärpfling / Furzer's Nothobranch
Ghona re Zou Game Reserve, Zimbabwe; B; 6,5 cm

▷♬◑☺☻⊡▨➠ ⚠⑤♂   _{Photo: L. Seegers}

_{Photo: L. Seegers}

A50050-4 *Nothobranchius fuscotaeniatus* Seegers, 1997 [Holotype]
Grüner Prachtgrundkärpfling / Green Nothobranch, "TZ 97/57"
2 km südlich der Ndundu-Fähre, Rufiji-Einzug, Ost-Tansania / 2 km S of Ndundu Ferry, Rufiji River drainage, Eastern Tanzania; W; 4,5 cm

⚠♬◑☺☻⊡▨➠ ◈⑤♂

A50050-4 *Nothobranchius fuscotaeniatus* Seegers, 1997
Grüner Prachtgrundkärpfling / Green Nothobranch, "TZ 97/57"
2 km S of Ndundu Ferry, Rufiji River drainage, E. Tanzania; W; 4,5 cm

⚠♬◑☺☻⊡▨➠ ◈⑤♂ ♀   _{Photo: L. Seegers}

A50050-4 *Nothobranchius fuscotaeniatus* Seegers, 1997
Grüner Prachtgrundkärpfling / Green Nothobranch, "TZ 97/57"
2 km S of Ndundu Ferry, Rufiji River drainage, E. Tanzania; W; 4,5 cm

⚠♬◑☺☻⊡▨➠ ◈⑤ ♀   _{Photo: L. Seegers}

A50070-3 *Nothobranchius guentheri* (PFEFFER, 1893)
Günthers Prachtgrundkärpfling / Guenther's Nothobranch
Near Amani Stadion, Zanzibar, Tanzania; W; 4,5 cm
⚠♨◑☺☹⬇️🐟➡◈⑤♂ Photo: L. Seegers

A50070-4 *Nothobranchius guentheri* (PFEFFER, 1893)
Günthers Prachtgrundkärpfling / Guenther's Nothobranch
Near Amani Stadion, Zanzibar, Tanzania; W; 4,5 cm
▷♨◑☺☹⬇️🐟➡⚠⑤♀ Photo: L. Seegers

A50071-3 *Nothobranchius guentheri* (PFEFFER, 1893)
Günthers Prachtgrundkärpfling / Guenther's Nothobranch
Goldform, Aquarienstamm / Golden Form, aquarium strain; B; 4,5 cm
⚠♨◑☺☹⬇️🐟➡◈⑤♂ Photo: L. Seegers

A50072-3 *Nothobranchius guentheri* (PFEFFER, 1893)
Günthers Prachtgrundkärpfling / Guenther's Nothobranch
Aquarienstamm / Aquarium strain; B; 4,5 cm
⚠♨◑☺☹⬇️🐟➡◈⑤♂ Photo: L. Seegers

A50087-4 *Nothobranchius interruptus* (PFEFFER, 1893)
Kikambala-Prachtgrundkärpfling / Kikambala Nothobranch
Kikambala, 15 km N Mombasa on road to Malindi, Kenya; W; 5 cm
⚠♨◑☺☹⬇️🐟➡◈⑤♂ Photo: L. Seegers

A50087-4 *Nothobranchius interruptus* (PFEFFER, 1893)
Kikambala-Prachtgrundkärpfling / Kikambala Nothobranch
Kikambala, 15 km N Mombasa on road to Malindi, Kenya; W; 5 cm
⚠♨◑☺☹⬇️🐟➡◈⑤♀ Photo: L. Seegers

A50088-4 *Nothobranchius interruptus* (PFEFFER, 1893)
Kikambala-Prachtgrundkärpfling / Kikambala Nothobranch
4 km inside at Kireme School, Kikambala N Mombasa, Kenya; W; 5 cm
⚠♨◑☺☹⬇️🐟➡◈⑤♂ Photo: L. Seegers

A50088-4 *Nothobranchius interruptus* (PFEFFER, 1893)
Kikambala-Prachtgrundkärpfling / Kikambala Nothobranch
4 km inside at Kireme School, Kikambala N Mombasa, Kenya; W; 5 cm
⚠♨◑☺☹⬇️🐟➡◈⑤♂ Photo: L. Seegers

A50090-4 *Nothobranchius janpapi* Wildekamp, 1977
Zwergprachtgrundkärpfling / Dwarf Nothobranch, "KTZ 85/34"
3 km S Bagamoyo / 3 km south of Bagamoyo, Tanzania; W; 3 cm
Photo: L. Seegers

A50091-4 *Nothobranchius janpapi* Wildekamp, 1977
Zwergprachtgrundkärpfling / Dwarf Nothobranch [T.t.]
Aquarium strain, Ruvu River 40 km W Dar es Salaam, Tanzania; B; 3 cm
Photo: L. Seegers

A50092-4 *Nothobranchius janpapi* Wildekamp, 1977
Zwergprachtgrundkärpfling / Dwarf Nothobranch, "TZ 91/105"
Ditch west of the Ruvu River, west of Bagamoyo, Tanzania; W; 3 cm
Photo: L. Seegers

A50092-4 *Nothobranchius janpapi* Wildekamp, 1977
Zwergprachtgrundkärpfling / Dwarf Nothobranch, "TZ 91/105"
Ditch west of the Ruvu River, west of Bagamoyo, Tanzania; W; 3 cm
Photo: L. Seegers

A50093-4 *Nothobranchius janpapi* Wildekamp, 1977
Zwergprachtgrundkärpfling / Dwarf Nothobranch, "TZ 82"
Rufiji River drainage on road to Selous Game Res., Tanzania; W; 3 cm
Photo: L. Seegers

A50094-4 *Nothobranchius janpapi* Wildekamp, 1977
Zwergprachtgrundkärpfling / Dwarf Nothobranch, "TZ 82"
F_1-mutation of the type strain from the Ruvu River, Tanzania; Z; 3 cm
Photo: L. Seegers

A50095-4 *Nothobranchius janpapi* Wildekamp, 1977
Zwergprachtgrundkärpfling / Dwarf Nothobranch, "TZ 97/57"
2 km S Ndundu Ferry, Rufiji drainage, Eastern Tanzania; W; 3 cm
Photo: L. Seegers

A50098-4 *Nothobranchius* spec. aff. *janpapi* Wildekamp, 1977
Zwergprachtgrundkärpfling / Dwarf Nothobranch, "TAN 95/4"
Kilombero swamp near Ifakara, Tanzania; B; 3 cm
Photo: L. Seegers

Nothobranchius janpapi WILDEKAMP, 1977 zeigen häufig ein von anderen Prachtgrundkärpflingen etwas abweichendes <u>5 Photos</u>: L. Seegers
Laichverhalten. Hier ein Wildfangpaar der Population "TZ 97/57" vom unteren Rufiji in Tanzania .

Nothobranchius janpapi WILDEKAMP, 1977 *may show a spawning behavior which is different from that of other* Nothobranchius *species. Here a wild caught pair of the population "TZ 97/57" from the lower Rufiji River in Tanzania is shown.*

Das Männchen nähert sich dem Weibchen in der freien Wassersäu-
le und versucht es von der Seite her mit den Flossen zu umgreifen.

*The male approaches the female in the free water column and tries to
embrace the partner with the dorsal and anal fins.*

Häufig wird bereits im freien Wasser in der Paarungshaltung abgelaicht. Die Tiere erstarren und sinken langsam nach unten.

*The pair already spawns frequently in the free water column. The
paralyzed fish slowly sink down.*

Wie bei anderen Arten wird die Afterflosse zur Tüte gefaltet. Während
dies das Ei sonst tief in den Boden bringt, fällt es hier frei auf den Boden.

*Like with other species the anal fin is folded to bring the egg deeply
into the ground. But in this species the egg freely fells down.*

Aber auch bei *Nothobranchius janpapi* kann das Paar - wie sonst in
der Gattung üblich - am Boden ablaichen.

*Nothobranchius janpapi, however, may also spawn as a bottom
spawner as it is done by most species within the genus.*

A50100-4 *Nothobranchius jubbi* WILDEKAMP & BERKENKAMP, 1979
Jubbs Prachtgrundkärpfling / Jubb's Nothobranch, "K 96/23"
Msumalini Creek, 29 km N Gongoni on road to Garsen, Kenya; W; 5 cm

Photo: L. Seegers

A50100-4 *Nothobranchius jubbi* WILDEKAMP & BERKENKAMP, 1979
Jubbs Prachtgrundkärpfling / Jubb's Nothobranch, "K 96/23"
Msumalini Creek, 29 km N Gongoni on road to Garsen, Kenya; W; 5 cm

Photo: L. Seegers

A50101-4 *Nothobranchius jubbi* WILDEKAMP & BERKENKAMP, 1979
Jubbs Prachtgrundkärpfling / Jubb's Nothobranch
4 km after Gongoni on Malindi - Garsen road, Kenya; W; 5 cm

Photo: L. Seegers

A50101-4 *Nothobranchius jubbi* WILDEKAMP & BERKENKAMP, 1979
Jubbs Prachtgrundkärpfling / Jubb's Nothobranch
4 km after Gongoni on Malindi - Garsen road, Kenya; W; 5 cm

Photo: L. Seegers

A50102-4 *Nothobranchius jubbi* WILDEKAMP & BERKENKAMP, 1979
Jubbs Prachtgrundkärpfling / Jubb's Nothobranch
Malindi, Kenia / Malindi, Kenya; W; 5 cm

Photo: L. Seegers

A50103-4 *Nothobranchius jubbi* WILDEKAMP & BERKENKAMP, 1979
Jubbs Prachtgrundkärpfling / Jubb's Nothobranch, "S 16"
Goba B, south of Kisimaio, Somalia; W; 5 cm

Photo: L. Seegers

A50104-4 *Nothobranchius jubbi* WILDEKAMP & BERKENKAMP, 1979
Jubbs Prachtgrundkärpfling / Jubb's Nothobranch, "S 8"
Shalanbod, Somalia; W; 5 cm

Photo: L. Seegers

A50105-4 *Nothobranchius jubbi* WILDEKAMP & BERKENKAMP, 1979
Jubbs Prachtgrundkärpfling / Jubb's Nothobranch, "S 13"
Azenda Bader, Somalia; W; 5 cm

Photo: L. Seegers

A50106-4 *Nothobranchius jubbi* WILDEKAMP & BERKENKAMP, 1979
Jubbs Prachtgrundkärpfling / Jubb's Nothobranch, "S 14"
Sunguni, Somalia; W; 5 cm

Photo: L. Seegers

A50107-4 *Nothobranchius jubbi* WILDEKAMP & BERKENKAMP, 1979
Jubbs Prachtgrundkärpfling / Jubb's Nothobranch, "S 16"
Durekalin, Somalia; W; 5 cm

Photo: L. Seegers

A50110-4 *Nothobranchius kafuensis* WILDEKAMP & ROSENSTOCK, 1989
Kafue Prachtgrundkärpfling / Kafue Nothobranch
Chunga, Sambia / Chunga, Zambia; W; 5,5 cm

Photo: L. Seegers

A50110-4 *Nothobranchius kafuensis* WILDEKAMP & ROSENSTOCK, 1989
Kafue Prachtgrundkärpfling / Kafue Nothobranch
Chunga, Sambia / Chunga, Zambia; W; 5,5 cm

Photo: L. Seegers

A50111-4 *Nothobranchius kafuensis* WILDEKAMP & ROSENSTOCK, 1989
Kafue Prachtgrundkärpfling / Kafue Nothobranch
Nega Nega, Sambia / Nega Nega, Zambia; W; 5,5 cm

Photo: L. Seegers

A50112-4 *Nothobranchius kafuensis* WILDEKAMP & ROSENSTOCK, 1989
Kafue Prachtgrundkärpfling / Kafue Nothobranch
Lochinvar, Sambia / Zambia; W; 5,5 cm

Photo: L. Seegers

A50113-4 *Nothobranchius kafuensis* WILDEKAMP & ROSENSTOCK, 1989
Kafue Prachtgrundkärpfling / Kafue Nothobranch
Kayuni State Farm, Sambia / Zambia, "red type"; B; 5,5 cm

Photo: L. Seegers

A50114-4 *Nothobranchius kafuensis* WILDEKAMP & ROSENSTOCK, 1989
Kafue Prachtgrundkärpfling / Kafue Nothobranch
Kayuni State Farm, Sambia / Zambia, "blue type"; B; 5,5 cm

Photo: L. Seegers

A50130-4 *Nothobranchius kirki* Jubb, 1969
Kirks Prachtgrundkärpfling / Kirk's Nothobranch
Aquarienstamm aus Malawi / Aquarium strain from Malawi; B; 4,5 cm
▷♫❶◑☺☹⬇☀➡ ◈⑤♂ Photo: L. Seegers

A50130-4 *Nothobranchius kirki* Jubb, 1969
Kirks Prachtgrundkärpfling / Kirk's Nothobranch
Aquarienstamm aus Malawi / Aquarium strain from Malawi; B; 4,5 cm
▷♫❶◑☺☹⬇☀➡ ◈⑤♂ Photo: R. Lütje

A50131-4 *Nothobranchius kirki* Jubb, 1969
Kirks Prachtgrundkärpfling / Kirk's Nothobranch
Chilwa-See, Malawi / Lake Chilwa, Malawi; B; 4,5 cm
▷♫❶◑☺☹⬇☀➡ ◈⑤♂ Photo: L. Seegers

A50130-3 *Nothobranchius kirki* Jubb, 1969
Kirks Prachtgrundkärpfling / Kirk's Nothobranch, "U 8"
Aquarienstamm aus Malawi / Aquarium strain from Malawi; B; 4,5 cm
▷♫❶◑☺☹⬇☀➡ ◈⑤♂ Photo: L. Seegers

A50132-4 *Nothobranchius* aff. *kirki* Jubb, 1969
Kirks Prachtgrundkärpfling / Kirk's Nothobranch
Sumpf, östlich Salima, Malawi / Swamp E Salima, Malawi; W; 4,5 cm
▷♫❶◑☺☹⬇☀➡ ◈⑤♂ Photo: W. Staeck

A50133-4 *Nothobranchius* aff. *kirki* Jubb, 1969
Kirks Prachtgrundkärpfling / Kirk's Nothobranch
Salima, Malawi; B; 4,5 cm
▷♫❶◑☺☹⬇☀➡ ◈⑤♂ Photo: L. Seegers

A50134-4 *Nothobranchius* aff. *kirki* Jubb, 1969
Kirks Prachtgrundkärpfling / Kirk's Nothobranch, "MW 94/3"
Benga, Malawi; B; 4,5 cm
▷♫❶◑☺☹⬇☀➡ ◈⑤♂ Photo: L. Seegers

A50134-4 *Nothobranchius* aff. *kirki* Jubb, 1969
Kirks Prachtgrundkärpfling / Kirk's Nothobranch, "MW 94/3"
Benga, Malawi; B; 4,5 cm
▷♫❶◑☺☹⬇☀➡ ◈⑤♀ Photo: L. Seegers

A50140-4 *Nothobranchius korthausae* Meinken, 1973
Mafia-Prachtgrundkärpfling / Mafia Nothobranch
Korthaus' strain from Mafia Island, Tanzania; W; 4,5 cm

⚠ 🐟 ◑ ☺ ☹ ⬇ 🖼 ➡ ◈ ⑤ ♂   _{Photo: L. Seegers}

A50141-4 *Nothobranchius korthausae* Meinken, 1973
Mafia-Prachtgrundkärpfling / Mafia Nothobranch, "brown form"
Eggers' strain from Mafia Island, Tanzania; W; 4,5 cm

⚠ 🐟 ◑ ☺ ☹ ⬇ 🖼 ➡ ◈ ⑤ ♂   _{Photo: L. Seegers}

A50142-4 *Nothobranchius korthausae* Meinken, 1973
Mafia-Prachtgrundkärpfling / Mafia Nothobranch, "red form"
Eggers' strain from Mafia Island, Tanzania; W; 4,5 cm

⚠ 🐟 ◑ ☺ ☹ ⬇ 🖼 ➡ ◈ ⑤ ♂   _{Photo: L. Seegers}

A50142-4 *Nothobranchius korthausae* Meinken, 1973
Mafia-Prachtgrundkärpfling / Mafia Nothobranch
Eggers' strain from Mafia Island, Tanzania; W; 4,5 cm

⚠ 🐟 ◑ ☺ ☹ ⬇ 🖼 ➡ ◈ ⑤ ♀   _{Photo: L. Seegers}

A50142-4 *Nothobranchius korthausae* Meinken, 1973
Mafia-Prachtgrundkärpfling / Mafia Nothobranch, "red form"
Eggers' strain from Mafia Island, Tanzania; F1; 4,5 cm

⚠ 🐟 ◑ ☺ ☹ ⬇ 🖼 ➡ ◈ ⑤ ♂   _{Photo: L. Seegers}

A50150-4 *Nothobranchius kuhntae* (Ahl, 1926)
Weinroter Prachtgrundkärpfling / Winered Nothobranch, "U 5"
Beira, Mozambique; B; 5 cm

⚠ 🐟 ◑ ☺ ☹ ⬇ 🖼 ➡ ◈ ⑤ ♂   _{Photo: L. Seegers}

A50151-4 *Nothobranchius kuhntae* (Ahl, 1926)
Weinroter Prachtgrundkärpfling / Winered Nothobranch
Roloffs Stamm / Roloff's strain, Beira, Mozambique; W; 5 cm

▷ 🐟 ◑ ☺ ☹ ⬇ 🖼 ➡ ◈ ⑤ ♂   _{Photo: E. Roloff}

A50152-4 *Nothobranchius kuhntae* (Ahl, 1926)
Weinroter Prachtgrundkärpfling / Winered Nothobranch, "Beira 1991"
Beira, Mozambique; B; 5 cm

▷ 🐟 ◑ ☺ ☹ ⬇ 🖼 ➡ ◈ ⑤ ♂   _{Photo: L. Seegers}

A50160-4 *Nothobranchius lourensi* WILDEKAMP, 1977
Lourens Prachtgrundkärpfling / Lourens' Nothobranch
Aquarium strain from the Ruvu River, Tanzania; B; 4,5 cm
 Photo: L. Seegers

A50160-3 *Nothobranchius lourensi* WILDEKAMP, 1977
Lourens Prachtgrundkärpfling / Lourens' Nothobranch
Aquarium strain from the Ruvu River, Tanzania; B; 4,5 cm
 Photo: L. Seegers

A50161-4 *Nothobranchius lourensi* WILDEKAMP, 1977
Lourens Prachtgrundkärpfling / Lourens' Nothobranch, "TZ 97/57"
2 km S of Ndundu Ferry, Rufiji River basin, E. Tanzania; W; 4,5 cm
Photo: L. Seegers

A50161-4 *Nothobranchius lourensi* WILDEKAMP, 1977
Lourens Prachtgrundkärpfling / Lourens' Nothobranch, "TZ 97/57"
2 km S of Ndundu Ferry, Rufiji River basin, E. Tanzania; W; 4,5 cm
Photo: L. Seegers

A50161-4 *Nothobranchius lourensi* WILDEKAMP, 1977
Lourens Prachtgrundkärpfling / Lourens' Nothobranch, "TZ 97/57"
2 km S of Ndundu Ferry, Rufiji River basin, E. Tanzania; W; 4,5 cm
Photo: L. Seegers

A50165-4 *Nothobranchius luekei* SEEGERS, 1984
Lükes Prachtgrundkärpfling / Lueke's Nothobranch, "TZ 83/5
Mbezi River, 40 km south of Dar es Salaam, Tanzania; B; 3,0 cm
Photo: L. Seegers

A50165-4 *Nothobranchius luekei* SEEGERS, 1984 [Holotype]
Lükes Prachtgrundkärpfling / Lueke's Nothobranch, "TZ 83/5"
Mbezi River, 40 km south of Dar es Salaam, Tanzania; W; 3,0 cm
Photo: L. Seegers

A50165-4 *Nothobranchius luekei* SEEGERS, 1984
Lükes Prachtgrundkärpfling / Lueke's Nothobranch, "TZ 83/5"
Mbezi River, 40 km south of Dar es Salaam, Tanzania; W; 3,0 cm
Photo: L. Seegers

A50050-4 *Nothobranchius* spec. "Makonde"
Makonde-Prachtgrundkärpfling / Makonde Nothobranch, "TZ 85/21"
Südost-Tanzania / Southeastern Tanzania; W; 5,0 cm
⚠ ♗ ◑ ☺ ☺ 🎲 📷 ➡ ◈ ⑤ ♂   Photo: L. Seegers

A50050-4 *Nothobranchius* spec. "Makonde"
Makonde-Prachtgrundkärpfling / Makonde Nothobranch, "TZ 85/21"
Südost-Tanzania / Southeastern Tanzania; W; 5,0 cm
⚠ ♗ ◑ ☺ ☺ 🎲 📷 ➡ ◈ ⑤ ♀   Photo: L. Seegers

A50051-4 *Nothobranchius* spec. "Makonde"
Makonde-Prachtgrundkärpfling / Makonde Nothobranch, "TZ 97/38"
Luwangula River W Puchapucha, Southern Tanzania; W; 5,0 cm
⚠ ♗ ◑ ☺ ☺ 🎲 📷 ➡ ◈ ⑤ ♂   Photo: L. Seegers

A50052-4 *Nothobranchius* spec. "Makonde"
Makonde-Prachtgrundkärpfling / Makonde Nothobranch, "TZ 97/43"
SW Maharunga, Ruvuma drainage, Southeastern Tanzania; W; 5,0 cm
⚠ ♗ ◑ ☺ ☺ 🎲 📷 ➡ ◈ ⑤ ♂   Photo: L. Seegers

A50180-4 *Nothobranchius melanospilus* (PFEFFER, 1896)
Schwarzflecken-Prachtgrundkärpfling / Black Spotted Nothobranch
Südost-Kenia / Southeastern Kenya; W; 8 cm
⚠ ♗ ◑ ☺ ☺ 🎲 📷 ➡ ◈ ⑤ ♂   Photo: L. Seegers

A50181-4 *Nothobranchius melanospilus* (PFEFFER, 1896)
Schwarzflecken-Prachtgrundkärpfling / Black Spotted Nothobranch
Nord-Sansibar, Tansania / Northern Zanzibar Island, Tanzania; W; 8 cm
⚠ ♗ ◑ ☺ ☺ 🎲 📷 ➡ ◈ ⑤ ♂   Photo: L. Seegers

A50182-4 *Nothobranchius melanospilus* (PFEFFER, 1896)
Schwarzflecken-Prachtgrundkärpfling / Black Spotted Nothobranch
"TZ 90/105", 40 km S Kidete on road Dodoma-Kilosa , Tanzania; W; 4,5 cm
⚠ ♗ ◑ ☺ ☺ 🎲 📷 ➡ ◈ ⑤ ♂   Photo: L. Seegers

A50182-4 *Nothobranchius melanospilus* (PFEFFER, 1896)
Schwarzflecken-Prachtgrundkärpfling / Black Spotted Nothobranch
"TZ 90/105", 40 km S Kidete on road Dodoma-Kilosa , Tanzania; W; 4,5 cm
⚠ ♗ ◑ ☺ ☺ 🎲 📷 ➡ ◈ ⑤ ♀   Photo: L. Seegers

Ablaichendes Paar von *Nothobranchius melanospilus* (Pfeffer, 1896) der Population "TZ 89/3" .

5 Photos: L. Seegers

Spawning pair of Nothobranchius melanospilus (Pfeffer, 1896) *of the population "TZ 89/3".*

Ein Männchen (oben) nimmt Kontakt zu einem Weibchen auf.

The male (top) approaches the female.

Das Weibchen sucht eine geeignete Ablaichstelle, wobei das Männchen ihm im Körperkontakt folgt.

Followed by the male the female looks for a suitable spawning site. The male keeps in contact with its partner.

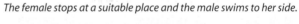

Das Weibchen hält an einer geeigneten Stelle an und das Männchen schwimmt neben die Partnerin.

The female stops at a suitable place and the male swims to her side.

Das Männchen "umgreift" den Hinterleib des Weibchens mit Rücken- und Afterflosse, beide pressen sich gegen den Boden.

The male "embraces" the female by its dorsal and anal fins, both fish are pressed against the soil.

Das Ei und die Spermien werden in den Boden abgegeben und das Paar trennt sich mit einem Ruck.

Egg and sperms are spawned into the soil and both fish push off the bottom.

A50183-4 *Nothobranchius melanospilus* (PFEFFER, 1896)
Schwarzflecken-Prachtgrundkärpfling / Black Spotted Nothobranch
"TZ 89/3", 16 km W Ruvu River W Bagamoyo, E Tanzania; W; 8 cm

Photo: L. Seegers

A50184-4 *Nothobranchius melanospilus* (PFEFFER, 1896)
Schwarzflecken-Prachtgrundkärpfling / Black Spotted Nothobranch
"TZ 91/105", Ruvu floodplain W of Bagamoyo , E Tanzania; W; 8 cm

Photo: L. Seegers

A50185-4 *Nothobranchius melanospilus* (PFEFFER, 1896)
Schwarzflecken-Prachtgrundkärpfling / Black Spotted Nothobranch
"TZ 89/101", South of Bagamoyo, Eastern Tanzania; W; 8 cm

Photo: L. Seegers

A50186-4 *Nothobranchius melanospilus* (PFEFFER, 1896)
Schwarzflecken-Prachtgrundkärpfling / Black Spotted Nothobranch
"TZ 94/1", Mbezi River, 40 km S Dar es Salaam, E Tanzania; W; 8 cm

Photo: L. Seegers

A50187-4 *Nothobranchius melanospilus* (PFEFFER, 1896)
Schwarzflecken-Prachtgrundkärpfling / Black Spotted Nothobranch
TZ 87/5, Lukware River S Dar es Salaam, Eastern Tanzania; W; 8 cm

Photo: L. Seegers

A50188-4 *Nothobranchius melanospilus* (PFEFFER, 1896)
Schwarzflecken-Prachtgrundkärpfling / Black Spotted Nothobranch
Mtanza, near northern entrance of Selous Game Res. , Tanzania; W; 8 cm

Photo: L. Seegers

A50189-4 *Nothobranchius melanospilus* (PFEFFER, 1896)
Schwarzflecken-Prachtgrundkärpfling / Black Spotted Nothobranch
TZ 97/48, Mihumo River, Mbwemkuru basin, S. Tanzania; W; 8 cm

Photo: L. Seegers

A50190-4 *Nothobranchius melanospilus* (PFEFFER, 1896)
Schwarzflecken-Prachtgrundkärpfling / Black Spotted Nothobranch
TZ 97/53, N Matandu River on Kilwa-Muhoro rd., S. Tanzania; W; 8 cm

Photo: L. Seegers

A50195-4 *Nothobranchius microlepis* (Vinciguerra, 1897)
Kleinschuppen-Prachtgrundkärpfling / Small Scaled Nothobranch
"S 5", Durbane, Somalia; W; 7 cm

⚠️🐟◑☺😄🎲🖼️➡️ ⚠️⑤♂ _{Photo: L. Seegers}

A50196-4 *Nothobranchius microlepis* (Vinciguerra, 1897)
Kleinschuppen-Prachtgrundkärpfling / Small Scaled Nothobranch
Tana-Ebene, Kenia / Tana River floodplain, Kenya; W; 7 cm

⚠️🐟◑☺😄🎲🖼️➡️ ⚠️⑤♂ _{Photo: L. Seegers}

A50200-4 *Nothobranchius neumanni* (Hilgendorf, 1905)
Neumanns Prachtgrundkärpfling / Neumann's Nothobranch
"TZ 82", Chipogola, Tanzania; W; 6 cm

▷🐟◑☺😄🎲🖼️➡️ ◈⑤♂ _{Photo: L. Seegers}

A50200-4 *Nothobranchius neumanni* (Hilgendorf, 1905)
Neumanns Prachtgrundkärpfling / Neumann's Nothobranch
"TZ 82", Chipogola, Tanzania; W; 6 cm

▷🐟◑☺😄🎲🖼️➡️ ◈⑤♀ _{Photo: L. Seegers}

A50200-4 *Nothobranchius neumanni* (Hilgendorf, 1905)
Neumanns Prachtgrundkärpfling / Neumann's Nothobranch
"TZ 82", Chipogola, Tanzania; W; 6 cm

▷🐟◑☺😄🎲🖼️➡️ ◈⑤♂ _{Photo: L. Seegers}

A50201-4 *Nothobranchius neumanni* (Hilgendorf, 1905)
Neumanns Prachtgrundkärpfling / Neumann's Nothobranch
Bubu system, 70 km from Dodoma on road to Mwanza, Tanzania; W; 6 cm

▷🐟◑☺😄🎲🖼️➡️ ◈⑤♂ _{Photo: L. Seegers}

A50202-4 *Nothobranchius neumanni* (Hilgendorf, 1905)
Neumanns Prachtgrundkärpfling / Neumann's Nothobranch
"TAN 78", Lake Manyara drainage, Tanzania; W; 6 cm

▷🐟◑☺😄🎲🖼️➡️ ◈⑤♂ _{Photo: L. Seegers}

A50202-4 *Nothobranchius neumanni* (Hilgendorf, 1905)
Neumanns Prachtgrundkärpfling / Neumann's Nothobranch
Lake Manyara drainage, Tanzania; W; 6 cm

▷🐟◑☺😄🎲🖼️➡️ ◈⑤♂ _{Photo: L. Seegers}

A50205-4 *Nothobranchius* sp. aff. *neumanni* (HILGENDORF, 1905)
Neumanns Prachtgrundkärpfling / Neumann's Nothobranch
"TZ 92/113", Malagarasi drain., Tabora-Mpanda rd., Tanzania; W; 6 cm
▷ ♫ ◐ ☺ ☹ ⬇ 🖼 🐛 ➡ ◈ ⑤ ♂   Photo: L. Seegers

A50205-4 *Nothobranchius* sp. aff. *neumanni* (HILGENDORF, 1905)
Neumanns Prachtgrundkärpfling / Neumann's Nothobranch
"TZ 92/113", Malagarasi drain., Tabora-Mpanda rd., Tanzania; W; 6 cm
▷ ♫ ◐ ☺ ☹ ⬇ 🖼 🐛 ➡ ◈ ⑤ ♀   Photo: L. Seegers

A50205-4 *Nothobranchius* sp. aff. *neumanni* (HILGENDORF, 1905)
Neumanns Prachtgrundkärpfling / Neumann's Nothobranch
"TZ 92/113", Malagarasi drain., Tabora-Mpanda rd., Tanzania; W; 6 cm
▷ ♫ ◐ ☺ ☹ ⬇ 🖼 🐛 ➡ ◈ ⑤ ♂   Photo: L. Seegers

A50206-4 *Nothobranchius* sp. aff. *neumanni* (HILGENDORF, 1905)
Neumanns Prachtgrundkärpfling / Neumann's Nothobranch
"TZ 92/149", Ruaha drainage on road to Mbeya, Tanzania; W; 6 cm
▷ ♫ ◐ ☺ ☹ ⬇ 🖼 🐛 ➡ ◈ ⑤ ♂   Photo: L. Seegers

A50206-4 *Nothobranchius* sp. aff. *neumanni* (HILGENDORF, 1905)
Neumanns Prachtgrundkärpfling / Neumann's Nothobranch
"TAN 76", Ruaha drainage at Ilonga on road to Mbeya, Tanzania; W; 6 cm
▷ ♫ ◐ ☺ ☹ ⬇ 🖼 🐛 ➡ ◈ ⑤ ♂   Photo: L. Seegers

A50207-4 *Nothobranchius* sp. aff. *neumanni* (HILGENDORF, 1905)
Neumanns Prachtgrundkärpfling / Neumann's Nothobranch
"TZ 88/17", Sinyanga, S Mbeya, Ruaha drainage, Tanzania; W; 6 cm
▷ ♫ ◐ ☺ ☹ ⬇ 🖼 🐛 ➡ ◈ ⑤ ♂   Photo: L. Seegers

A50210-4 *Nothobranchius orthonotus* (PETERS, 1844)
Mozambique-Prachtgrundkärpfling / Mozambique Nothobranch
Pongolo River, South African Republik; B; 8 cm
▷ ♫ ◐ ☺ ☹ ⬇ 🖼 🐛 ➡ ◈ ⑤ ♂   Photo: L. Seegers

A50211-4 *Nothobranchius orthonotus* (PETERS, 1844)
Mozambique-Prachtgrundkärpfling / Mozambique Nothobranch
Krüger National Park, South African Republik; B; 8 cm
▷ ♫ ◐ ☺ ☹ ⬇ 🖼 🐛 ➡ ◈ ⑤ ♂   Photo: L. Seegers

A50215-4 *Nothobranchius palmqvisti* (LÖNNBERG, 1907)
Palmqvists Prachtgrundkärpfling / Palmqvist's Nothobranch
Mrima, SO-Kenia / Mrima, SE Kenya; W; 4,5 cm

Photo: L. Seegers

A50215-4 *Nothobranchius palmqvisti* (LÖNNBERG, 1907)
Palmqvists Prachtgrundkärpfling / Palmqvist's Nothobranch
Mrima, SO-Kenia / Mrima, SE Kenya; W; 4,5 cm

Photo: L. Seegers

A50216-4 *Nothobranchius palmqvisti* (LÖNNBERG, 1907)
Palmqvists Prachtgrundkärpfling / Palmqvist's Nothobranch
"TZ 94/7", 14 km W Pangani on road to Muheza, Tanzania; W; 4,5 cm

Photo: L. Seegers

A50217-4 *Nothobranchius palmqvisti* (LÖNNBERG, 1907)
Palmqvists Prachtgrundkärpfling / Palmqvist's Nothobranch
Aquarienstamm / Aquarium strain; B; 4,5 cm

Photo: G. Kopic

A50220-4 *Nothobranchius patrizii* (VINCIGUERRA, 1927)
Somalia-Prachtgrundkärpfling / Somalia Nothobranch, "K 96/23"
Msumalini Creek, 29 km N Gongoni, E Kenya; W; 4,5 cm

Photo: L. Seegers

A50221-4 *Nothobranchius patrizii* (VINCIGUERRA, 1927)
Somalia-Prachtgrundkärpfling / Somalia Nothobranch
Giohar, Somalia; W; 4,5 cm

Photo: L. Seegers

A50222-4 *Nothobranchius patrizii* (VINCIGUERRA, 1927)
Somalia-Prachtgrundkärpfling / Somalia Nothobranch
Warfa, Somalia; B; 4,5 cm

Photo: L. Seegers

A50222-4 *Nothobranchius patrizii* (VINCIGUERRA, 1927)
Somalia-Prachtgrundkärpfling / Somalia Nothobranch
Warfa, Somalia; B; 4,5 cm

Photo: L. Seegers

A50225-4 *Nothobranchius polli* Wildekamp, 1978
Polls Prachtgrundkärpfling / Poll's Nothobranch
Lubumbashi, Shaba, Zaïre; W; 5 cm
Photo: R. Wildekamp

A50225-4 *Nothobranchius polli* Wildekamp, 1978
Polls Prachtgrundkärpfling / Poll's Nothobranch, strain of 1960
Lubumbashi, Shaba, Zaïre; W; 5 cm
Photo: A. v. d. Nieuwenhuizen

A50230-4 *Nothobranchius rachovii* Ahl, 1926
Rachows Prachtgrundkärpfling / Rachow's Nothobranch
Aquarienstamm "rot" / Aquarium strain "red"; B; 5 cm
Photo: L. Seegers

A50230-4 *Nothobranchius rachovii* Ahl, 1926
Rachows Prachtgrundkärpfling / Rachow's Nothobranch
Aquarienstamm "rot" / Aquarium strain "red"; B; 5 cm
Photo: L. Seegers

A50231-4 *Nothobranchius rachovii* Ahl, 1926
Rachows Prachtgrundkärpfling / Rachow's Nothobranch
Beira, Mozambique, 1991; B; 5 cm
Photo: R. Wildekamp

A50232-4 *Nothobranchius rachovii* Ahl, 1926
Rachows Prachtgrundkärpfling / Rachow's Nothobranch
Aquarienstamm "blau" / Aquarium strain "blue"; B; 5 cm
Photo: J. Tomas

A50233-4 *Nothobranchius rachovii* Ahl, 1926
Rachows Prachtgrundkärpfling / Rachow's Nothobranch
Krüger National Park, South African Republic; B; 5 cm
Photo: L. Seegers

A50233-4 *Nothobranchius rachovii* Ahl, 1926
Rachows Prachtgrundkärpfling / Rachow's Nothobranch
Krüger National Park, South African Republic; B; 5 cm
Photo: L. Seegers

A50235-4 *Nothobranchius robustus* AHL, 1935
Roter Prachtgrundkärpfling / Red Nothobranch, "K 86/13"
Sio River, Kenia / Sio River, Kenya; W; 4 cm

Photo: L. Seegers

A50235-4 *Nothobranchius robustus* AHL, 1935
Roter Prachtgrundkärpfling / Red Nothobranch, "K 86/13"
Sio River, Kenia / Sio River, Kenya; W; 4 cm

Photo: L. Seegers

A50236-4 *Nothobranchius robustus* AHL, 1935
Roter Prachtgrundkärpfling / Red Nothobranch, "UG 90/11"
2 km S Kalisizo, West-Uganda; W; 4 cm

Photo: R. Wildekamp

A50237-4 *Nothobranchius robustus* AHL, 1935
Roter Prachtgrundkärpfling / Red Nothobranch, "UG 90/15"
W Mubende, Uganda; W; 4 cm

Photo: R. Wildekamp

A50240-4 *Nothobranchius rubripinnis* SEEGERS, 1935
Rotflossen-Prachtgrundkärpfling / Red Finned Nothobranch
"TZ 83/5", Mbezi River, O-Tansania / Mbezi River, E Tanzania; W; 4 cm

Photo: L. Seegers

A50240-4 *Nothobranchius rubripinnis* SEEGERS, 1935
Rotflossen-Prachtgrundkärpfling / Red Finned Nothobranch
"TZ 83/5", Mbezi River, O-Tansania / Mbezi River, E Tanzania; W; 4 cm

Photo: L. Seegers

A50241-4 *Nothobranchius rubripinnis* SEEGERS, 1935
Rotflossen-Prachtgrundkärpfling / Red Finned Nothobranch
"TZ 94/1", Mbezi River, O-Tansania / Mbezi River, E Tanzania; W; 4 cm

Photo: L. Seegers

A50241-4 *Nothobranchius rubripinnis* SEEGERS, 1935
Rotflossen-Prachtgrundkärpfling / Red Finned Nothobranch
"TZ 94/1", Mbezi River, O-Tansania / Mbezi River, E Tanzania; W; 4 cm

Photo: L. Seegers

A50245-4 *Nothobranchius* spec. "Rovuma"
Rovuma-Prachtgrundkärpfling / Rovuma Nothobranch, "KTZ 85/20"
Mindu near Nakapanya, E Tunduru, SE Tanzania; W; 6 cm
▷ ♫ ◑ ☺ ☹ ⬆ 🖼 🐟 ➤ ◈ ⑤ ♂
Photo: L. Seegers

A50245-4 *Nothobranchius* spec. "Rovuma"
Rovuma-Prachtgrundkärpfling / Rovuma Nothobranch, "KTZ 85/20"
Mindu near Nakapanya, E Tunduru, SE Tanzania; W; 6 cm
▷ ♫ ◑ ☺ ☹ ⬆ 🖼 🐟 ➤ ◈ ⑤ ♀
Photo: L. Seegers

A50245-4 *Nothobranchius* spec. "Rovuma"
Rovuma-Prachtgrundkärpfling / Rovuma Nothobranch, "KTZ 85/20"
Mindu near Nakapanya, E Tunduru, SE Tanzania; W; 6 cm
▷ ♫ ◑ ☺ ☹ ⬆ 🖼 🐟 ➤ ◈ ⑤ ♂ ♀
Photo: L. Seegers

A50246-4 *Nothobranchius* spec. "Rovuma"
Rovuma-Prachtgrundkärpfling / Rovuma Nothobranch, "TZ 97/39"
Nakapanya, E Tunduru, Muhowesi drainage, SE Tanzania; W; 6 cm
▷ ♫ ◑ ☺ ☹ ⬆ 🖼 🐟 ➤ ◈ ⑤ ♂
Photo: L. Seegers

A50250-4 *Nothobranchius steinforti* WILDEKAMP, 1977
Steinforts Prachtgrundkärpfling / Steinfort's Nothobranch
Aquarium strain from near Kimamba, SE Tanzania; B; 5 cm
⚠ ♫ ◑ ☺ ☹ ⬆ 🖼 🐟 ➤ ◈ ⑤ ♂
Photo: L. Seegers

A50250-4 *Nothobranchius steinforti* WILDEKAMP, 1977
Steinforts Prachtgrundkärpfling / Steinfort's Nothobranch
Aquarium strain from near Kimamba, SE Tanzania; B; 5 cm
⚠ ♫ ◑ ☺ ☹ ⬆ 🖼 🐟 ➤ ◈ ⑤ ♀
Photo: L. Seegers

A50250-4 *Nothobranchius steinforti* WILDEKAMP, 1977
Steinforts Prachtgrundkärpfling / Steinfort's Nothobranch
Aquarium strain from near Kimamba, SE Tanzania; B; 5 cm
⚠ ♫ ◑ ☺ ☹ ⬆ 🖼 🐟 ➤ ◈ ⑤ ♂
Photo: L. Seegers

A50255-4 *Nothobranchius symoensi* WILDEKAMP, 1978
Symoens Prachtgrundkärpfling / Symoens' Nothobranch, "ZAM 92/2"
Kapalala, Sambia / Kapalala, Zambia; B; 5 cm
⚠ ♫ ◑ ☺ ☹ ⬆ 🖼 🐟 ➤ ◈ ⑤ ♂
Photo: R. Wildekamp

A50260-4 *Nothobranchius taeniopygus* HILGENDORF, 1891
Gestreifter Prachtgrundkärpfling / Striped Nothobranch, "KTZ 85/9"
Kazi Kazi, W Itigi, Central Tanzania; W; 6 cm
▷ ₧ ◑ ☺ ☺ ⊡ ⊠ ➥ ◈ ⑤ ♂   Photo: L. Seegers

A50261-4 *Nothobranchius taeniopygus* HILGENDORF, 1891
Gestreifter Prachtgrundkärpfling / Striped Nothobranch
Bujora, Mwanza area, Lake Victoria drainage, Tanzania; B; 6 cm
▷ ₧ ◑ ☺ ☺ ⊡ ⊠ ➥ ◈ ⑤ ♂   Photo: L. Seegers

A50262-4 *Nothobranchius taeniopygus* HILGENDORF, 1891
Gestreifter Prachtgrundkärpfling / Striped Nothobranch, "TZ 92/5"
55 km NW Tabora on road to Nzega, Central Tanzania; F1; 6 cm
▷ ₧ ◑ ☺ ☺ ⊡ ⊠ ➥ ◈ ⑤ ♂   Photo: L. Seegers

A50262-4 *Nothobranchius taeniopygus* HILGENDORF, 1891
Gestreifter Prachtgrundkärpfling / Striped Nothobranch, "TZ 92/5"
55 km NW Tabora on road to Nzega, Central Tanzania; F1; 6 cm
▷ ₧ ◑ ☺ ☺ ⊡ ⊠ ➥ ◈ ⑤ ♀   Photo: L. Seegers

A50263-4 *Nothobranchius taeniopygus* HILGENDORF, 1891
Gestreifter Prachtgrundkärpfling / Striped Nothobranch, "TZ 92/6"
31 km S Nzega on road to Tabora, Central Tanzania; W; 6 cm
▷ ₧ ◑ ☺ ☺ ⊡ ⊠ ➥ ◈ ⑤ ♂   Photo: L. Seegers

A50264-4 *Nothobranchius taeniopygus* HILGENDORF, 1891
Gestreifter Prachtgrundkärpfling / Striped Nothobranch, "TZ 92/8"
46 km NW Kahama, Central Tanzania; W; 6 cm
▷ ₧ ◑ ☺ ☺ ⊡ ⊠ ➥ ◈ ⑤ ♂   Photo: L. Seegers

A50265-4 *Nothobranchius taeniopygus* HILGENDORF, 1891
Gestreifter Prachtgrundkärpfling / Striped Nothobranch, "TZ 94/131"
Limba Limba, on Kitunda-Tabora road, Central Tanzania; W; 6 cm
▷ ₧ ◑ ☺ ☺ ⊡ ⊠ ➥ ◈ ⑤ ♂   Photo: L. Seegers

A50266-4 *Nothobranchius taeniopygus* HILGENDORF, 1891
Gestreifter Prachtgrundkärpfling / Striped Nothobranch, "TZ 94/132"
31 km S Ipole on Kitunda-Tabora road, Central Tanzania; W; 6 cm
▷ ₧ ◑ ☺ ☺ ⊡ ⊠ ➥ ◈ ⑤ ♂   Photo: L. Seegers

A50267-4 *Nothobranchius taeniopygus* Hilgendorf, 1891
Gestreifter Prachtgrundkärpfling / Striped Nothobranch, "TZ 94/102"
Nkululu River on Itigi-Rungwa road, Western Tanzania; W; 6 cm
▷♫◑☺☹⬆️🔲➡️ ◈⑤♂
Photo: L. Seegers

A50268-4 *Nothobranchius taeniopygus* Hilgendorf, 1891
Gestreifter Prachtgrundkärpfling / Striped Nothobranch, "TZ 94/104"
Ipati River E of Inyonga, Western Tanzania; W; 6 cm
▷♫◑☺☹⬆️🔲➡️ ◈⑤♂
Photo: L. Seegers

A50269-4 *Nothobranchius taeniopygus* Hilgendorf, 1891
Gestreifter Prachtgrundkärpfling / Striped Nothobranch, "KTZ 85/5"
Kondoa/Irangi, Central Tanzania; W; 6 cm
▷♫◑☺☹⬆️🔲➡️ ◈⑤♂
Photo: L. Seegers

A50269-4 *Nothobranchius taeniopygus* Hilgendorf, 1891
Gestreifter Prachtgrundkärpfling / Striped Nothobranch, "KTZ 85/5"
Kondoa/Irangi, Central Tanzania; W; 6 cm
▷♫◑☺☹⬆️🔲➡️ ◈⑤♀
Photo: L. Seegers

A50275-4 *Nothobranchius ugandensis* Wildekamp, 1994
Uganda-Prachtgrundkärpfling / Ugandan Nothobranch, "UG 88/8"
Uganda; F1; 6 cm
▷♫◑☺☹⬆️🔲➡️ ◈⑤♂
Photo: L. Seegers

A50276-4 *Nothobranchius ugandensis* Wildekamp, 1994
Uganda-Prachtgrundkärpfling / Ugandan Nothobranch, "U 88/18"
106 km N Kampala, Uganda; W; 6 cm
▷♫◑☺☹⬆️🔲➡️ ◈⑤♂
Photo: L. Seegers

A50277-4 *Nothobranchius ugandensis* Wildekamp, 1994
Uganda-Prachtgrundkärpfling / Ugandan Nothobranch, "U 88/19"
92 km N Kampala, Uganda; W; 6 cm
▷♫◑☺☹⬆️🔲➡️ ◈⑤♂
Photo: L. Seegers

A50277-4 *Nothobranchius ugandensis* Wildekamp, 1994
Uganda-Prachtgrundkärpfling / Ugandan Nothobranch, "U 88/19"
92 km N Kampala, Uganda; W; 6 cm
▷♫◑☺☹⬆️🔲➡️ ◈⑤♀
Photo: L. Seegers

A50280-4 *Nothobranchius vosseleri* Aʜʟ, 1924
Pangani-Prachtgrundkärpfling / Pangani Nothobranch, "TAN 95/19"
Mombo, Pangani-Einzug, Ost-Tansania / E Tanzania; B; 6 cm
⚠ ♈ ◐ ☺ ☻ ⬛ 🖾 ➡ ◈ ⑤ ♂   Photo: L. Seegers

A50281-4 *Nothobranchius vosseleri* Aʜʟ, 1924
Pangani-Prachtgrundkärpfling / Pangani Nothobranch, "TZ 97/7"
Kifaru, Pangani drainage, Ost-Tansania / E Tanzania; W; 6 cm
⚠ ♈ ◐ ☺ ☻ ⬛ 🖾 ➡ ◈ ⑤ ♂   Photo: L. Seegers

A50282-4 *Nothobranchius vosseleri* Aʜʟ, 1924
Pangani-Prachtgrundkärpfling / Pangani Nothobranch, "TAN 95/18"
NW Korogwe, Ost-Tansania / E Tanzania; B; 6 cm
⚠ ♈ ◐ ☺ ☻ ⬛ 🖾 ➡ ◈ ⑤ ♂   Photo: L. Seegers

A50282-4 *Nothobranchius vosseleri* Aʜʟ, 1924
Pangani-Prachtgrundkärpfling / Pangani Nothobranch, "TAN 95/18"
NW Korogwe, Ost-Tansania / E Tanzania; B; 6 cm
⚠ ♈ ◐ ☺ ☻ ⬛ 🖾 ➡ ◈ ⑤ ♀   Photo: L. Seegers

A50283-4 *Nothobranchius vosseleri* Aʜʟ, 1924
Pangani-Prachtgrundkärpfling / Pangani Nothobranch, "TZ 97/5"
Korogwe, Pangani-Einzug, Ost-Tansania / E Tanzania; W; 6 cm
⚠ ♈ ◐ ☺ ☻ ⬛ 🖾 ➡ ◈ ⑤ ♂   Photo: L. Seegers

A50284-4 *Nothobranchius vosseleri* Aʜʟ, 1924
Pangani-Prachtgrundkärpfling / Pangani Nothobranch, "TAN 95/17"
Südlich Korogwe, Pangani-Einzug, Ost-Tansania / E Tanzania; B; 6 cm
⚠ ♈ ◐ ☺ ☻ ⬛ 🖾 ➡ ◈ ⑤ ♂   Photo: L. Seegers

A50290-4 *Nothobranchius* spec. "Lake Victoria"
Viktoria-Prachtgrundkärpfling / Victoria Nothobranch, "K 86/9"
Odienya, SW Ahero, Lake Victoria drainage, Kenya; W; 4,5 cm
⚠ ♈ ◐ ☺ ☻ ⬛ 🖾 ➡ ◈ ⑤ ♂   Photo: L. Seegers

A50290-4 *Nothobranchius* spec. "Lake Victoria"
Viktoria-Prachtgrundkärpfling / Victoria Nothobranch, "K 86/9"
Odienya, SW Ahero, Lake Victoria drainage, Kenya; W; 4,5 cm
⚠ ♈ ◐ ☺ ☻ ⬛ 🖾 ➡ ◈ ⑤ ♂ ♀   Photo: L. Seegers

A50291-4 *Nothobranchius* spec. "Lake Victoria"
Viktoria-Prachtgrundkärpfling / Victoria Nothobranch
Mugeta, N Serengeti, Lake Victoria drainage, Tanzania; B; 4,5 cm
⚠🚰◑☺☺☹⬇️🖼➡ ◈🆂♂ Photo: L. Seegers

A50295-4 *Nothobranchius willerti* Wᴉʟᴅᴇᴋᴀᴍᴘ, 1992
Tana-Prachtgrundkärpfling / Tana Nothobranch
Mnanzini, Tana-Einzug, Kenia / Tana drainage, Kenya; W; 4,5 cm
⚠🚰◑☺☺☹⬇️🖼➡ ◈🆂♂ Photo: L. Seegers

A50300-4 *Nothobranchius* sp. aff. *rubripinnis* Sᴇᴇɢᴇʀs, 1986
Mbwemkuru-Prachtgrundkärpfling / Mbwemkuru Nothobranch
"KTZ 85/28", near Mbwemkuru River, Lindi-Kilwa road, Tanzania; W; 4 cm
⚠🚰◑☺☺☹⬇️🖼➡ ⚠🆂♂ Photo: L. Seegers

A50300-4 *Nothobranchius* sp. aff. *rubripinnis* Sᴇᴇɢᴇʀs, 1986
Mbwemkuru-Prachtgrundkärpfling / Mbwemkuru Nothobranch
"KTZ 85/28", near Mbwemkuru River, Lindi-Kilwa road, Tanzania; F₁; 4 cm
⚠🚰◑☺☺☹⬇️🖼➡ ⚠🆂♂ Photo: L. Seegers

A50305-4 *Nothobranchius* spec. "Ifakara"
Ifakara-Prachtgrundkärpfling / Ifakara Nothobranch, "TAN 95/4"
Ifakara, Kilombero, Rufiji River drainage, Tanzania; B; 4 cm
⚠🚰◑☺☺☹⬇️🖼➡ ⚠🆂♂ Photo: L. Seegers

A50305-4 *Nothobranchius* spec. "Ifakara"
Ifakara-Prachtgrundkärpfling / Ifakara Nothobranch, "TAN 95/4"
Ifakara, Kilombero, Rufiji River drainage, Tanzania; B; 4 cm
⚠🚰◑☺☺☹⬇️🖼➡ ⚠🆂♂ Photo: L. Seegers

A50310-4 *Nothobranchius* spec. "Limba Limba"
Malagarasi-Prachtgrundkärpfling / Malagarasi Nothobranch, "TZ 94/131"
Limba Limba, south of Tabora, Tanzania; W; 5 cm
▷🚰◑☺☺☹⬇️🖼➡ ⚠🆂♂ Photo: L. Seegers

A50310-4 *Nothobranchius* spec. "Limba Limba"
Malagarasi-Prachtgrundkärpfling / Malagarasi Nothobranch, "TZ 94/131"
Limba Limba, south of Tabora, Tanzania; W; 5 cm
▷🚰◑☺☺☹⬇️🖼➡ ⚠🆂♀ Photo: L. Seegers

A50315-4 *Nothobranchius* spec. "Caprivi Strip"
Caprivi-Prachtgrundkärpfling / Caprivi Nothobranch, "95/1"
Caprivi Strip, Namibia; B; 5 cm
Photo: L. Seegers

A50315-4 *Nothobranchius* spec. "Caprivi Strip"
Caprivi-Prachtgrundkärpfling / Caprivi Nothobranch, "95/1"
Caprivi Strip, Namibia; B; 5 cm
Photo: L. Seegers

A50320-4 *Nothobranchius* spec. "Kisaki"
Kisaki-Prachtgrundkärpfling / Kisaki Nothobranch, "TAN 95/5"
Kisaki, south of Uluguru Mountains, E-Tanzania; B; 5 cm
Photo: L. Seegers

A50325-4 *Nothobranchius* spec. "Ruvu"
Ruvu-Prachtgrundkärpfling /Ruvu Nothobranch "TZ 89/3"
16 km W Ruvu River W Bagamoyo , Tanzania; W; 4,5 cm
Photo: L. Seegers

A50326-4 *Nothobranchius* spec. "Ruvu"
Ruvu-Prachtgrundkärpfling /Ruvu Nothobranch "TZ 91/103"
Ruvu floodplain W Bagamoyo , Tanzania; W; 4,5 cm
Photo: L. Seegers

A50326-4 *Nothobranchius* spec. "Ruvu"
Ruvu-Prachtgrundkärpfling /Ruvu Nothobranch "TZ 91/103"
Ruvu floodplain W Bagamoyo , Tanzania; W; 4,5 cm
Photo: L. Seegers

A50330-4 *Nothobranchius furzeri*
x *Nothobranchius kuhntae*
Kreuzung / Crossbreed; B; 6 cm
Photo: L. Seegers

A50331-4 *Nothobranchius guentheri*
x *Nothobranchius rubripinnis*, "TZ 83/5"
Kreuzung / Crossbreed; B; 4,5 cm
Photo: L. Seegers

A51910-4 *Pachypanchax omalonotus* (DUMÉRIL, 1861)
Madagaskar-Hechtling / Madagascar Panchax
Nossy Bé, "blau", Madagaskar / Nossy Bé, "blue", Madagascar; W; 7 cm
▷♫◑☺☹⊞🖼➡ ◈⑤♂   Photo: L. Seegers

A51911-4 *Pachypanchax omalonotus* (DUMÉRIL, 1861)
Madagaskar-Hechtling / Madagascar Panchax
Nossy Bé, "rot", Madagaskar / Nossy Bé, "red", Madagascar; W; 7 cm
▷♫◑☺☹⊞🖼➡ ◈⑤♂   Photo: L. Seegers

A51912-4 *Pachypanchax omalonotus* (DUMÉRIL, 1861)
Madagaskar-Hechtling / Madagascar Panchax
Abania, Madagaskar / Abania, Madagascar; B; 7 cm
▷♫◑☺☹⊞🖼➡ ◈⑤♂   Photo: E. Schraml

A51913-4 *Pachypanchax omalonotus* (DUMÉRIL, 1861)
Madagaskar-Hechtling / Madagascar Panchax
Nossy Bé, Madagaskar / Nossy Bé, Madagascar; B; 7 cm
▷♫◑☺☹⊞🖼➡ ◈⑤♀   Photo: R. Wildekamp

A51615-4 *Pachypanchax playfairii* (GÜNTHER, 1866)
Seychellen-Hechtling / Playfair's Panchax, Seychelles Panchax
Aquarienstamm / Aquarium strain; B; 7 cm
▷♫◑☺☹⊞🖼➡ ◈⑤♂   Photo: L. Seegers

A51916-4 *Pachypanchax playfairii* (GÜNTHER, 1866)
Seychellen-Hechtling / Playfair's Panchax, Seychelles Panchax
Marahubi Palace, Zanzibar, Tanzania; W; 7 cm
▷♫◑☺☹⊞🖼➡ ◈⑤♂   Photo: L. Seegers

A51920-4 *Pachypanchax sakaramyi* (HOLLY, 1928) (valid species?)
Sakaramy-Hechtling / Sakaramy Panchax
Sakaramy, Nord-Madagaskar / Sakaramy, northern Madagascar; B; 7 cm
▷♫◑☺☹⊞🖼➡ ◈⑤♂   Photo: L. Seegers

A51920-4 *Pachypanchax sakaramyi* (HOLLY, 1928) (valid species?)
Sakaramy-Hechtling / Sakaramy Panchax
Sakaramy, Nord-Madagaskar / Sakaramy, northern Madagascar; B; 7 cm
▷♫◑☺☹⊞🖼➡ ◈⑤♀   Photo: L. Seegers

A53705-4 *Paranothobranchius ocellatus* SEEGERS, 1985
Hechtlings-Prachtgrundkärpfling / Pike Panchax
Ruvu drainage W Bagamoyo, Tanzania; W; 14 cm

Photo: L. Seegers

A53705-4 *Paranothobranchius ocellatus* SEEGERS, 1985
Hechtlings-Prachtgrundkärpfling / Pike Panchax
Ruvu drainage W Bagamoyo, Tanzania; W; 14 cm

Photo: L. Seegers

A53706-4 *Paranothobranchius ocellatus* SEEGERS, 1985
Hechtlings-Prachtgrundkärpfling / Pike Panchax
Mtanza near northern gate of Selous Game Res., Tanzania; B; 14 cm

Photo: L. Seegers

A53706-3 *Paranothobranchius ocellatus* SEEGERS, 1985 [Paratype]
Hechtlings-Prachtgrundkärpfling / Pike Panchax
Mtanza near northern gate of Selous G.R., Tanzania; W; 14 cm

Photo: L. Seegers

A75105-4 *Pronothobranchius kiyawensis* (AHL, 1928)
Kiyawa-Prachtgrundkärpfling / Kiyawa Nothobranch
Accra-Ebene, SO Ghana / Accra plains, SE Ghana; B; 3,5 cm

Photo: L. Seegers

A75105-4 *Pronothobranchius kiyawensis* (AHL, 1928)
Kiyawa-Prachtgrundkärpfling / Kiyawa Nothobranch
Accra-Ebene, SO Ghana / Accra plains, SE Ghana; B; 4 cm

Photo: S. Hellner

A75105-4 *Pronothobranchius kiyawensis* (AHL, 1928)
Kiyawa-Prachtgrundkärpfling / Kiyawa Nothobranch
Accra-Ebene, SO Ghana / Accra plains, SE Ghana; B; 4 cm

Photo: S. Hellner

A75105-4 *Pronothobranchius kiyawensis* (AHL, 1928)
Kiyawa-Prachtgrundkärpfling / Kiyawa Nothobranch
Accra-Ebene, SO Ghana / Accra plains, SE Ghana; B; 4 cm

Photo: S. Hellner

 © Verlag A.C.S. GmbH

Photo: L. Seegers

1. *Rivulus xiphidius*
2. *Trigonectes* spec. aus Bolivien
   Trigonectes *spec. from Bolivia*

Photo: H. Linke

Diese und alle anderen in
These and all others in

Aqua**log**
reference fish of the world

Killifishes of the World **New World Killis**

Aphaniidae
& Valenciidae

Photo: R. Wildekamp

Photo: R. Wildekamp

Photo: H. Wischmann

1. Abflußbach von Quelle 3, Aci Gölü, Türkei. Hier lebt *Aphanius anatoliae transgrediens*.
2. Oberer Ceyhan Nehri Fluß in West-Elbistan, Türkei. Biotop von *Aphanius mento*.
3. In diesem Bach im Stadtgebiet von Peniscola, Spanien, leben die in der Existenz bedrohten *Aphanius iberus* und *Valencia hispanica*.

1. Effluent of spring 3, Aci Gölü, Türkei where *Aphanius anatoliae transgrediens* can be collected.
2. Upper Ceyhan Nehri River in West-Elbistan, Türkei. Habitat of *Aphanius mento*.
3. In this brook in Peniscola, Spain, the threatened *Aphanius iberus* und *Valencia hispanica* co-occur.

E15005-4 *Aphanius anatoliae anatoliae* (LEIDENFROST, 1912)
Anatolienkärpfling / Anatolian Killi
Aksaray, Türkei / Turkey; W; 5,0-5,5 cm
▽♫↑P○☺☹⊕⊞▦➜⚠ⓜ♂   Photo: L. Seegers

E15005-4 *Aphanius anatoliae anatoliae* (LEIDENFROST, 1912)
Anatolienkärpfling / Anatolian Killi
Aksaray, Türkei / Turkey; W; 5,0-5,5 cm
▽♫↑P○☺☹⊕⊞▦➜⚠ⓜ♀   Photo: L. Seegers

E15006-4 *Aphanius anatoliae anatoliae* (LEIDENFROST, 1912)
Anatolienkärpfling / Anatolian Killi
Pinarbasi, Türkei / Turkey; B; 5,0-5,5 cm
▽♫↑P○☺☹⊕⊞▦➜⚠ⓜ♂   Photo: L. Seegers

E15006-4 *Aphanius anatoliae anatoliae* (LEIDENFROST, 1912)
Anatolienkärpfling / Anatolian Killi
Pinarbasi, Türkei / Turkey; B; 5,0-5,5 cm
▽♫↑P○☺☹⊕⊞▦➜⚠ⓜ♀   Photo: L. Seegers

E15010-4 *Aphanius anatoliae splendens* (KOSSWIG & SÖZER, 1945)
Glänzender Anatolienkärpfling / Gölçük Anatolian Killi, "T 92/15"
Salda Gölü, Türkei / Turkey; W; 5,5-6,0 cm
▽♫↑P○☺☹⊕⊞▦➜⚠ⓜ♂   Photo: R. Wildekamp

E15010-4 *Aphanius anatoliae splendens* (KOSSWIG & SÖZER, 1945)
Glänzender Anatolienkärpfling / Gölçük Anatolian Killi, "T 92/15"
Salda Gölü, Türkei / Turkey; W; 5,5-6,0 cm
▽♫↑P○☺☹⊕⊞▦➜⚠ⓜ♀   Photo: R. Wildekamp

E15015-4 *Aphanius anatoliae sureyanus* (NEU, 1937)
Burdur-Anatolienkärpfling / Lake Burdur Killi
Burdur Gölü, Türkei / Turkey; W; 5,0-5,5 cm
▽♫↑P○☺☹⊕⊞▦➜⚠ⓜ♂   Photo: R. Wildekamp

E15015-4 *Aphanius anatoliae sureyanus* (NEU, 1937)
Burdur-Anatolienkärpfling / Lake Burdur Killi
Burdur Gölü, Türkei / Turkey; W; 5,0-5,5 cm
▽♫↑P○☺☹⊕⊞▦➜⚠ⓜ♀   Photo: R. Wildekamp

E15020-4 *Aphanius anatoliae transgrediens* (ERMIN, 1946)
Acigöl-Anatolienkärpfling / Acigöl Killi
Spring 3, Akpinar, Aci Gölü, Türkei / Turkey; B; 4,5-5,0 cm
▽🅱ⁱ🅿○☺☻☹⊕⊕⊞💠➡ ⚠🔳 ♂   Photo: L. Seegers

E15020-4 *Aphanius anatoliae transgrediens* (ERMIN, 1946)
Acigöl-Anatolienkärpfling / Acigöl Killi
Spring 3, Akpinar, Aci Gölü, Türkei / Turkey; B; 4,5-5,0 cm
▽🅱ⁱ🅿○☺☻☹⊕⊕⊞💠➡ ⚠🔳 ♀   Photo: L. Seegers

E15025-4 *Aphanius (Tellia) apodus* (GERVAIS, 1853)
Atlaskärpfling / Atlas Killi
Ain M'Lila, Algerien / Algeria; B; 4,5-5,0 cm
▽🅱ⁱ🅿○☺☻☹⊕⊕⊞💠➡ ⚠🔳 ♂   Photo: L. Seegers

E15025-4 *Aphanius (Tellia) apodus* (GERVAIS, 1853)
Atlaskärpfling / Atlas Killi
Ain M'Lila, Algerien / Algeria; B; 4,5-5,0 cm
▽🅱ⁱ🅿○☺☻☹⊕⊕⊞💠➡ ⚠🔳 ♀   Photo: L. Seegers

E15026-4 *Aphanius (Tellia) apodus* (GERVAIS, 1853)
Atlaskärpfling / Atlas Killi
Hochland von Constantine, Algerien / Algeria; B; 4,5-5,0 cm
▽🅱ⁱ🅿○☺☻☹⊕⊕⊞💠➡ ⚠🔳 ♂   Photo: L. Seegers

E15026-4 *Aphanius (Tellia) apodus* (GERVAIS, 1853)
Atlaskärpfling / Atlas Killi
Hochland von Constantine, Algerien / Algeria; B; 4,5-5,0 cm
▽🅱ⁱ🅿○☺☻☹⊕⊕⊞💠➡ ⚠🔳 ♀   Photo: L. Seegers

E15030-4 *Aphanius (Kosswigichthys) asquamatus* (SÖZER, 1942)
Nacktschuppen-Anatolienkärpfling / Hazer Gölü Killi
Hazer Gölü, Türkei / Turkey; W; 4,0 cm
▽🅱ⁱ🅿○☺☻☹⊕⊕⊞💠➡ ⚠🔳 ♂   Photo: L. Seegers

E15030-4 *Aphanius (Kosswigichthys) asquamatus* (SÖZER, 1942)
Nacktschuppen-Anatolienkärpfling / Hazer Gölü Killi
Hazer Gölü, Türkei / Turkey; W; 4,0 cm
▽🅱ⁱ🅿○☺☻☹⊕⊕⊞💠➡ ⚠🔳 ♀   Photo: L. Seegers

E15035-4 *Aphanius chantrei* (GAILLARD, 1895)
Östlicher Anatolienkärpfling / Eastern Anatolian Killi
Karpuzatan, 10 km N Kaiseri, Türkei / Turkey; W; 6,0-7,0 cm
▽▷♨⇞○☺☻☹✪⊞🐌➾ ⚠🄜 ♂   Photo: L. Seegers

E15035-4 *Aphanius chantrei* (GAILLARD, 1895)
Östlicher Anatolienkärpfling / Eastern Anatolian Killi
Karpuzatan, 10 km N Kaiseri, Türkei / Turkey; W; 6,0-7,0 cm
▽▷♨⇞○☺☻☹✪⊞🐌➾ ⚠🄜 ♀   Photo: L. Seegers

E15036-4 *Aphanius chantrei* (GAILLARD, 1895)
Östlicher Anatolienkärpfling / Eastern Anatolian Killi
Kirkgöz, Türkei / Turkey; W; 6,0-7,0 cm
▽▷♨⇞○☺☻☹✪⊞🐌➾ ⚠🄜 ♂   Photo: L. Seegers

E15036-4 *Aphanius chantrei* (GAILLARD, 1895)
Östlicher Anatolienkärpfling / Eastern Anatolian Killi
Kirkgöz, Türkei / Turkey; W; 6,0-7,0 cm
▽▷♨⇞○☺☻☹✪⊞🐌➾ ⚠🄜 ♀   Photo: L. Seegers

E15037-4 *Aphanius chantrei* (GAILLARD, 1895)
Östlicher Anatolienkärpfling / Eastern Anatolian Killi
Soysali, Türkei / Turkey; W; 6,0-7,0 cm
▽▷♨⇞○☺☻☹✪⊞🐌➾ ⚠🄜 ♂   Photo: E. Schraml

E15040-4 *Aphanius dispar dispar* (RÜPPELL, 1829)
Perlmutterkärpfling / Arabian Killifish
Scusciuban, Nord-Somalia / Northern Somalia; W; 6,0-7,0 cm
⚠⇞○☺☻☹✪⊞🐌➾ ⚠🄜🄛 ♂   Photo: L. Seegers

E15041-4 *Aphanius dispar dispar* (RÜPPELL, 1829)
Perlmutterkärpfling / Arabian Killifish
Iran; W; 6,0-7,0 cm
⚠⇞○☺☻☹✪⊞🐌➾ ⚠🄜🄛 ♂   Photo: L. Seegers

E15041-4 *Aphanius dispar dispar* (RÜPPELL, 1829)
Perlmutterkärpfling / Arabian Killifish
Iran; W; 6,0-7,0 cm
⚠⇞○☺☻☹✪⊞🐌➾ ⚠🄜🄛 ♀   Photo: L. Seegers

E15042-4 *Aphanius dispar dispar* (Rüppell, 1829)
Perlmutterkärpfling / Arabian Killifish
Dubai; W; 6,0-7,0 cm
⚠ ⚲P ○ ☺ ☻ ⊕ ⊞ 🗔 ➤ ⚠ ⊞ 🗔 ♂
Photo: S. Hellner

E15042-4 *Aphanius dispar dispar* (Rüppell, 1829)
Perlmutterkärpfling / Arabian Killifish
Dubai; W; 6,0-7,0 cm
⚠ ⚲P ○ ☺ ☻ ⊕ ⊞ 🗔 ➤ ⚠ ⊞ 🗔 ♀
Photo: S. Hellner

E15045-4 *Aphanius dispar richardsoni* (Boulenger, 1907)
Israel-Perlmutterkärpfling / Arabian Killifish
Ein Fashka, West-Jordanien /Western Jordan; W; 6,0-7,0 cm
⚠ ⚲P ○ ☺ ☻ ⊕ ⊞ 🗔 ➤ ⚠ ⊞ 🗔 ♂
Photo: L. Seegers

E15045-4 *Aphanius dispar richardsoni* (Boulenger, 1907)
Israel-Perlmutterkärpfling / Arabian Killifish
Ein Fashka, West-Jordanien /Western Jordan; W; 6,0-7,0 cm
⚠ ⚲P ○ ☺ ☻ ⊕ ⊞ 🗔 ➤ ⚠ ⊞ 🗔 ♀
Photo: L. Seegers

E15050-4 *Aphanius fasciatus* (Valenciennes in Humboldt &
Mittelmeerkärpfling / Mediterranean Killifish   Valenciennes, 1821)
Korfu, Griechenland / Korfu, Greece; W; 6,0-7,0 cm
▽ ⚠ ⚲P ○ ☺ ☻ ⊕ ⊞ 🗔 ➤ ⚠ 🗔 ♂
Photo: L. Seegers

E15050-4 *Aphanius fasciatus* (Valenciennes in Humboldt &
Mittelmeerkärpfling / Mediterranean Killifish   Valenciennes, 1821)
Korfu, Griechenland / Korfu, Greece; W; 6,0-7,0 cm
▽ ⚠ ⚲P ○ ☺ ☻ ⊕ ⊞ 🗔 ➤ ⚠ 🗔 ♀
Photo: L. Seegers

E15051-4 *Aphanius fasciatus* (Valenciennes in Humboldt &
Mittelmeerkärpfling / Mediterranean Killifish   Valenciennes, 1821)
Cagliari, Sardinien / Cagliari, Sardinia; W; 6,0-7,0 cm
▽ ⚠ ⚲P ○ ☺ ☻ ⊕ ⊞ 🗔 ➤ ⚠ 🗔 ♂
Photo: L. Seegers

E15052-4 *Aphanius fasciatus* (Valenciennes in Humboldt &
Mittelmeerkärpfling / Mediterranean Killifish   Valenciennes, 1821)
Ost-Algerien / Eastern Algeria; W; 6,0-7,0 cm
▽ ⚠ ⚲P ○ ☺ ☻ ⊕ ⊞ 🗔 ➤ ⚠ 🗔 ♂
Photo: L. Seegers

E15055-4 *Aphanius iberus* (Valenciennes in Cuvier & Valenciennes, 1846)
Spanienkärpfling / Spanish Killifish
Cartagena, Spanien / Cartagena, Spain; W; 4,5-5,0 cm
▽▷⇂P○☺☹⊕⊞🖼🐟 ⚠🔟 ♂
Photo: L. Seegers

E15055-4 *Aphanius iberus* (Valenciennes in Cuvier & Valenciennes, 1846)
Spanienkärpfling / Spanish Killifish
Cartagena, Spanien / Cartagena, Spain; W; 4,5-5,0 cm
▽▷⇂P○☺☹⊕⊞🖼🐟 ⚠🔟 ♀
Photo: L. Seegers

E15056-4 *Aphanius iberus* (Valenciennes in Cuvier & Valenciennes, 1846)
Spanienkärpfling / Spanish Killifish
Ebro-Delta, Spanien / Delta of Ebro River, Spain; W; 4,5-5,0 cm
▽▷⇂P○☺☹⊕⊞🖼🐟 ⚠🔟 ♂
Photo: L. Seegers

E15057-4 *Aphanius iberus* (Valenciennes in Cuvier & Valenciennes, 1846)
Spanienkärpfling / Spanish Killifish
Estartit, Spanien / Estartit, Spain; W; 4,5-5,0 cm
▽▷⇂P○☺☹⊕⊞🖼🐟 ⚠🔟 ♂
Photo: L. Seegers

E15058-4 *Aphanius iberus* (Valenciennes in Cuvier & Valenciennes, 1846)
Spanienkärpfling / Spanish Killifish
Peniscola, Spanien / Peniscola, Spain; W; 4,5-5,0 cm
▽▷⇂P○☺☹⊕⊞🖼🐟 ⚠🔟 ♂
Photo: L. Seegers

E15059-4 *Aphanius iberus* (Valenciennes in Cuvier & Valenciennes, 1846)
Spanienkärpfling / Spanish Killifish
Santa Pola, Spanien / Santa Pola, Spain; B; 4,5-5,0 cm
▽▷⇂P○☺☹⊕⊞🖼🐟 ⚠🔟 ♂
Photo: L. Seegers

E15060-4 *Aphanius iberus* (Valenciennes in Cuvier & Valenciennes, 1846)
Spanienkärpfling / Spanish Killifish
Valencia, Spanien / Valencia, Spain; W; 4,5-5,0 cm
▽▷⇂P○☺☹⊕⊞🖼🐟 ⚠🔟 ♂
Photo: L. Seegers

E15061-4 *Aphanius iberus* (Valenciennes in Cuvier & Valenciennes, 1846)
Spanienkärpfling / Spanish Killifish
Igli, Wadi Saoura, NW-Algerien / NW Algeria; W; 4,5-5,0 cm
▽▷⇂P○☺☹⊕⊞🖼🐟 ⚠🔟 ♂
Photo: L. Seegers

E15065-4 *Aphanius mento* (Heckel in Russegger, 1843)
Orientkärpfling / Black Persian Minnow
Ein Fashka, Totes Meer / Ein Fashka, Dead Sea, Israel; W; 5,0-6,0 cm
▽▷♫↿P○☺☺☻⊕⊞▨➤ ⚠▥ ♂ Photo: L. Seegers

E15065-4 *Aphanius mento* (Heckel in Russegger, 1843)
Orientkärpfling / Black Persian Minnow
Ein Fashka, Totes Meer / Ein Fashka, Dead Sea, Israel; W; 5,0-6,0 cm
▽▷♫↿P○☺☺☻⊕⊞▨➤ ⚠▥ ♀ Photo: L. Seegers

E15066-4 *Aphanius mento* (Heckel in Russegger, 1843)
Orientkärpfling / Black Persian Minnow
Israel / Israel; B; 5,0-6,0 cm
▽▷♫↿P○☺☺☻⊕⊞▨➤ ⚠▥ ♂ Photo: L. Seegers

E15067-4 *Aphanius mento* (Heckel in Russegger, 1843)
Orientkärpfling / Black Persian Minnow
Kirkgöz, Türkei / Kirkgöz, Turkey; W; 5,0-6,0 cm
▽▷♫↿P○☺☺☻⊕⊞▨➤ ⚠▥ ♂ Photo: L. Seegers

E15068-4 *Aphanius mento* (Heckel in Russegger, 1843)
Orientkärpfling / Black Persian Minnow
Südliche Türkei / Southern Turkey; W; 5,0-6,0 cm
▽▷♫↿P○☺☺☻⊕⊞▨➤ ⚠▥ ♂ Photo: L. Seegers

E15068-4 *Aphanius mento* (Heckel in Russegger, 1843)
Orientkärpfling / Black Persian Minnow
Südliche Türkei / Southern Turkey; W; 5,0-6,0 cm
▽▷♫↿P○☺☺☻⊕⊞▨➤ ⚠▥ ♀ Photo: L. Seegers

E15070-4 *Aphanius sirhani* (Villwock, Scholl & Krupp, 1983)
Azraqkärpfling / Azraq Killifish
Oase Azraq, Jordanien / Azraq Oasis, Jordan; B; 4,5-5,0 cm
▽▷♫↿P○☺☺☻⊕⊞▨➤ ⚠▥ ♂ Photo: L. Seegers

E15070-4 *Aphanius sirhani* (Villwock, Scholl & Krupp, 1983)
Azraqkärpfling / Azraq Killifish
Oase Azraq, Jordanien / Azraq Oasis, Jordan; B; 4,5-5,0 cm
▽▷♫↿P○☺☺☻⊕⊞▨➤ ⚠▥ ♀ Photo: L. Seegers

E15075-4 *Aphanius sophiae* (HECKEL in RUSSEGGER, 1846)
Persienkärpfling / Persian Minnow
Persepolis, Iran / Persepolis, Iran; B; 4,0-4,5 cm
▽▷♫⇡P○☺☻⊕⊞🔲➡ ⚠🔲 ♂　Photo: L. Seegers

E15075-4 *Aphanius sophiae* (HECKEL in RUSSEGGER, 1846)
Persienkärpfling / Persian Minnow
Persepolis, Iran / Persepolis, Iran; B; 4,0-4,5 cm
▽▷♫⇡P○☺☻⊕⊞🔲➡ ⚠🔲 ♀　Photo: L. Seegers

E88305-4 *Valencia hispanica* (VALENCIENNES in CUVIER & VALENCIENNES, 1846)
Valenciakärpfling / Spanish Toothcarp, Valencia Minnow
Valencia, Spanien / Valencia, Spain; W; 6,0-7,0 cm
▽▷♫○☺☻⊞🔲➡ ⚠🔲 ♂　Photo: L. Seegers

E88305-4 *Valencia hispanica* (VALENCIENNES in CUVIER & VALENCIENNES, 1846)
Valenciakärpfling / Spanish Toothcarp, Valencia Minnow
Valencia, Spanien / Valencia, Spain; W; 6,0-7,0 cm
▽▷♫○☺☻⊞🔲➡ ⚠🔲 ♀　Photo: L. Seegers

E88306-4 *Valencia hispanica* (VALENCIENNES in CUVIER & VALENCIENNES, 1846)
Valenciakärpfling / Spanish Toothcarp, Valencia Minnow
Peniscola, Spanien / Peniscola, Spain; W; 6,0-7,0 cm
▽▷♫○☺☻⊞🔲➡ ⚠🔲 ♂　Photo: L. Seegers

E88306-4 *Valencia hispanica* (VALENCIENNES in CUVIER & VALENCIENNES, 1846)
Valenciakärpfling / Spanish Toothcarp, Valencia Minnow
Peniscola, Spanien / Peniscola, Spain; W; 6,0-7,0 cm
▽▷♫○☺☻⊞🔲➡ ⚠🔲 ♂　Photo: L. Seegers

E88310-4 *Valencia letourneuxi* (SAUVAGE, 1880)
Korfu-Kärpfling / Korfu Minnow
Korfu, Griechenland / Korfu, Greece; W; 6,0-6,5 cm
▽▷♫○☺☻⊞🔲➡ ⚠🔲 ♂　Photo: L. Seegers

E88310-4 *Valencia letourneuxi* (SAUVAGE, 1880)
Korfu-Kärpfling / Korfu Minnow
Korfu, Griechenland / Korfu, Greece; W; 6,0-6,5 cm
▽▷♫○☺☻⊞🔲➡ ⚠🔲 ♂　Photo: L. Seegers

E15056-4 *Aphanius iberus* (Valenciennes in Cuvier & Valenciennes, 1846)
Spanienkärpfling / Spanish Killifish
Ebro-Delta, Spanien / Delta of Ebro River, Spain; W; 4,5-5,0 cm

Photo: L. Seegers

E15069-4 *Aphanius mento*, territoriales Männchen einer Aquarienpopulation unbekannter Herkunft.
Aphanius mento, territorial male of an aquarium strain of unknown origin.

Photo: H.-J. Richter/
Archiv ACS

**Ergänzungen/*Stickups*
hier einkleben**

erhältlich zusammen mit Ihrer
Aqualog*news*
der ersten internationalen Zeitung
für den Aquarianer

Aqualog *Bücher & Zeitung*
Jetzt auch im Net:

http:// www. aqualog. de
mit Informationen zu den Ergänzungen
und Neuerscheinungen

**Supplements/stickups
Please attach here**

Stickups are available in
Aqualog*news*
the international newspaper for aquarists

Aqualog *books & news*
now in the Internet

http:// www. aqualog. de
the latest information on supplements
and new publications

Ergänzungen/*Stickups*
hier einkleben

erhältlich zusammen mit Ihrer
Aqualognews
der ersten internationalen Zeitung
für den Aquarianer

Aqualog *Bücher & Zeitung*
jetzt auch im Net:

http:// www. aqualog. de
mit Informationen zu den Ergänzungen
und Neuerscheinungen

Supplements/stickups
Please attach here

Stickups are available in
Aqualognews
the international newspaper for aquarists

Aqualog *books & news*
now in the Internet

http:// www. aqualog. de
the latest information on supplements
and new publications

Ergänzungen/*Stickups*
hier einkleben

erhältlich zusammen mit Ihrer
Aqualognews
der ersten internationalen Zeitung
für den Aquarianer

Aqualog *Bücher & Zeitung*
jetzt auch im Net:

http:// www. aqualog. de
mit Informationen zu den Ergänzungen
und Neuerscheinungen

Supplements/stickups
Please attach here

Stickups are available in
Aqualognews
the international newspaper for aquarists

Aqualog *books & news*
now in the Internet

http:// www. aqualog. de
the latest information on supplements
and new publications

INDEX
alphabetisch / alphabetic

INDEX
alphabetisch / alphabetic

INDEX
alphabetisch / alphabetic

Literaturhinweise
Bibliography

AHL, E.   (1924a):   Zur Systematik der Altweltlichen Zahnkarpfen der Unterfamilie Fundulinae. – Zool. Anz., 60 (1-2): 49-55.
—   (1924b):   Über neue afrikanische Zahnkarpfen der Gattung *Panchax*. – Zool. Anz., 60 (3-4): 303-312.
ARNOLD, J.P. (1906):   Über den Ursprung der neuen *Haplochilus panchax*-Varietäten. – Wochenschr. Aquar. Terrar. Kde., 3 (52): 635-638.
—   (1907):   Nochmals die neuen *Panchax*-Varietäten. – Blätter Aquar. Terr. Kde., 18 (8): 77-78.
—   (1911):   Der Formen- und Farbenkreis der *Haplochilus panchax*-Gruppe. – Wochenschr. Aquar. Terr. Kde., 8 (46): 669-672.
ARNOLD, J.P. & E. AHL (1936): Fremdländische Süßwasserfische. – Gustav Wenzel & Sohn, Braunschweig. 529 pp.
BAENSCH, H.A., & R. RIEHL (1993): Aquarien-Atlas, Band 2 (6. Aufl.). – Mergus Verlag, Melle.
—   (1995):   Aquarien-Atlas, Band 4. – Mergus Verlag, Melle.
—   (1997):   Aquarien-Atlas, Band 5. – Mergus Verlag, Melle.
BERKENKAMP, H.O. & V. ETZEL (1986): Revision der asiatischen Gattung *Aplocheilus* McClelland, 1839 (Familie Aplocheilidae Bleeker, 1860). – Deutsche Killifisch Gemeinschaft, Journal, 18 (3): 32-43; (5): 57-70.
BIANCO, P.G., & R.R. MILLER (1989): First record of *Valencia letourneuxi* (Sauvage, 1880) in Peloponnese (Greece) and remarks on the Mediterranean family Valenciidae (Cyprinodontiformes). – Cybium, 13 (4): 385-387.
BOULENGER, G.A. (1903): On the fishes collected by Mr. G.L. Bates in southern Cameroon. – Proc. Zool. Soc. London, 1903 (1): 21-29, plates.
—   (1908):   Description of two new Cyprinodontid fishes from west Africa. – Ann. Mag. Nat. Hist., ser. 8, 2 (7): 29-30.
—   (1915):   Catalogue of the fresh-water fishes of Africa in the British Museum (Natural History). – The British Museum (Natural History), London, Vol. 3: i-xii+1-526, figures.
CLAUSEN, H.S. (1967): Tropical Old World cyprinodonts. – Akademisk Forlag, Kopenhagen. 64 pp.
DAGET, J. (1962):   Les poissons du Fouta Dialon et de la Basse Guinée. – Mém. Inst. fr. Afr. Noire (I.F.A.N.), 65: 210 pp., figs, pls.
ETZEL, V. (1996):   Bemerkungen zur systematischen Einordnung von *Epiplatys infrafasciatus, Epiplatys sexfasciatus* und *Epiplatys togolensis* unter besonderer Berücksichtigung der Abhängigkeit ihrer Verbreitung von den Regenwaldgebieten. – Deutsche Killifisch Gemeinschaft, Journal, 28 (5): 65-80.
GARMAN, S. (1895):   The Cyprinodonts. – Mem. Mus. Comp. Zoöl. Harvard Coll., 19 (1): 1-179, Pl. I-XII.

GÓMEZ CARUANA, F., S. PEIRO GÓMEZ & S. SÁNCHEZ ARTAL (1984): Descripcion de una nueva especie de pez continental iberico, *Valencia lozanoi* n. sp. (Pisces, Cyprinodontidae). – Boletín de la Estación Central de Ecología, **13** (25): 67-74.

HOLLY, M. (1930): Synopsis der Süßwasserfische Kameruns. – Sitzber. Akad. Wiss. Wien, I. Abt., Math.-nat. Kl., **139** (3-4): 195-281, figs., pls.

HUBER, J.H. (1978): Contribution à la connaissance des Cyprinodontidés de l'Afrique occidentale. – Rev. fr. Aquariol., **5** (1): 29 pp., 46 figs., map.

–   (1980): Rapport sur la deuxième expédition au Gabon (Août '79). Étude des Cyprinodontidés récoltes. – Rev. fr. Aquariol., **7** (2): 37-42, 10 figs.

–   (1982): Rapport de synthèse sur l'expédition au Congo (1978). Cyprinodontidés récoltés et *Micropanchax sylvestris* synonyme de *stictopleuron*. – Rev. fr. Aquariol., **9** (1): 1-12, figs.

HUBER, J.H. & A.C. RADDA (1977): Cyprinodontiden-Studien in Gabun. 4. Das Du Chaillu Massiv. – Aquaria, **24**: 99-110, 10 figs., map.

KLAUSEWITZ, W. (1957): Neue Süßwasserfische aus Thailand. – Senckenb. Biol., **38** (3-4): 196-199, fig.

KÖHLER, W. (1906): Diesjährige Neuheiten in Wort und Bild. 1. Neue Farbvarietäten der *Panchax*-Gruppe. – Blätter Aquar. Terr. Kde., **17** (39): 383-391.

–   (1907): Die neuen *Panchax*-Varietäten. Erste und letzte Entgegnung an Herrn Paul Arnold, Hamburg. – Blätter Aquar. Terr. Kde., **18** (2): 16-19.

LANGTON, R.W. (1996): Wild Collections of Killifish 1950-1995. – American Killifish Association. Second Edition, pp. 1-70.

LAZARA, K.J. (1984): Killifish Master Index (3rd ed.). – American Killifish Association, Cincinnati. 295 pp.

–   (1987): *Diapteron*, Gattung oder Untergattung? – Deutsche Killifisch Gemeinschaft, Journal, **19** (6): 92-96; (7): 109-112.

MEINKEN, H. (1932): Über einige neue Zahnkarpfen aus dem tropischen Westafrika. – Blätter Aquar. Terrar.-Kde, **43** (4): 53-58.

–   (1964): *Aplocheilus panchax rubropunctatus* subspec. nov., eine hübsche indische Cyprinodontiden-Neuheit (Pisces; Cyprinodontidae). – Die Aquar. Terrar. Z. (DATZ), **17** (5): 146-148, figs.

MYERS, G.S. (1924): A new poeciliid fish from the Congo, with remarks on Funduline genera. – Amer. Mus. Novitates, **116**: 1-9.

PETERS, N. (1963): Embryonale Anpassungen oviparer Zahnkarpfen aus periodisch autrocknenden Gewässern. – Int. Revue ges. Hydrobiol., **48** (2): 257-313.

RADDA, A. (1969): *Fundulosoma thierryi* und ihre Verwandten (Cyprinodontiformes, Rivulinae). – Aquaria, **16** (3): 159-164, figs.

RADDA, A.C., & E. PÜRZL (1987): Colour Atlas of Cyprinodonts of the Rain Forests of Tropical Africa. – Verlag Otto Hofmann, Wien. 160 pp.

SCHEEL, J.J. (1968): Rivulins of the Old World. – T.F.H. Publications, Jersey City, N.J., USA.

–   (1990): Atlas of Killifishes of the Old World. – T.F.H. Publications, Neptune City, NJ., USA.

SCHEEL, J.J. & R. ROMAND (1981): A New Genus of Rivulin Fish from Tropical Africa (Pisces, Cyprinodontidae). – Trop. Fish Hobb., **29** (11): 22-30, 7 figs.

SEEGERS, L. (1980): Killifische. Eierlegende Zahnkarpfen im Aquarium. Verlag Eugen Ulmer, Stuttgart.

–   (1985): Prachtgrundkärpflinge. Die Gattung *Nothobranchius*: Systematik, Vorkommen, Pflege und Zucht. – Deutsche Killifisch Gemeinschaft, Journal, Supplementheft No. 1: 1-48, figs.

–   (1986): Bemerkungen über die Sammlung der Cyprinodontiformes (Pisces: Teleostei) des Zoologischen Museums Berlin. I. Die Gattungen *Aphyosemion* Myers, 1924 und *Fundulosoma* Ahl, 1924. Teil 1. – Mitt. Zool. Mus. Berlin, **62** (2): 303-321.

–   (1988): Bemerkungen über die Sammlung der Cyprinodontiformes (Pisces: Teleostei) des Zoologischen Museums Berlin. I. Die Gattungen *Aphyosemion* Myers, 1924 und *Fundulosoma* Ahl, 1924. Teil 2. – Mitt. Zool. Mus. Berlin, **64** (1): 3-70.

–   (1996): The Fishes of the Lake Rukwa Drainage. – Ann. Mus. r. Afr. centr. Tervuren, Sci. Zool., **278**: 407 pp., 281 figs., drawings.

–   (1997): Killifishes of the World. Old World Killis I. – Aqualog, Vol. 7: 1-160, A.C.S. Verlag.

SETHI, R.P. (1960): Osteology and phylogeny of oviparous cyprinodont fishes (order Cyprinodontiformes). – Ph.D. dissertation, Univ. Florida, Univ. Microfilms, Ann Arbor: 1-275.

SMITH, H.M. (1938): On the genera *Aplocheilus* and *Panchax*. – Proc. Biol. Soc. Washington, **51**: 165-166.

STENGLEIN, W. (1993): *Epiplatys sexfasciatus infrafasciatus*? Was verbirgt sich unter diesem Namen? – Das Aquarium, **27** (289): 15-18.

TERCEIRA, A.C. (1974): Killifish. Their care and breeding. – Pisces Publishing Corporation, Belden Station Norwalk, CT, USA. 140 pp.

VILLWOCK, W. (1977): Das Genus *Aphanius* Nardo, 1827. – Deutsche Killifisch Gemeinschaft, Journal, **9** (11): 165-185.

WILDEKAMP, R. (1982): Prachtkärpflinge. – Alfred Kernen Verlag/Reimar Hobbing Verlag, Essen.

–   (1993): A World of Killies. Atlas of the Oviparous Cyprinodontiform Fishes of the World. Vol. 1. – The American Killifish Assoc.

–   (1995): A World of Killies. Atlas of the Oviparous Cyprinodontiform Fishes of the World. Vol. 2. – The American Killifish Assoc.

WILDEKAMP, R.H. & R. HAAS (1992): Redescription of *Nothobranchius microlepis*, description of two new species from northern Kenya and southern Somalia, and note on the status of *Paranothobranchius* (Cyprinodontiformes: Aplocheilidae). – Ichthyol. Explor. Freshwaters, **3** (1): 1-16.

Das weltweit anerkannte System,
The renowned AQUALOG system -
unentbehrlich für Handel,
used worldwide by importe

- Aqualog Special zeigen Ihnen jeweils die populärsten und schönsten Fische

- Gleichzeitig ein dekoratives Poster

- Mit informativem Text und Pflegeanleitung

- AQUALOG Specials - presenting the most popular and beautiful fishes of one group

- Each special makes a beautiful fold-up poster

- Includes an informative introduction and care instructions

special;

X40255-4 Colisa lalia - Red Roter Zwergfadenfisch / Red Dwarf Gourami Breeding Form, B, 6 cm

X94025-4 Trichopsis pumila (Arnold, 1936) Knurrender Zwerggurami / Pygmy Gourami Thailand, Malaysia, Indonesia, W, 4 cm
Photo: Archiv ACS Migge / Reinhard

Das vollständige Bildlexikon.....
The complete reference work .....

- Abonnieren Sie die erste und einzige internationale Zeitung für Aquarianer

- 4-farbig mit vielen aktuellen Informationen

- Stickups zum Einkleben aktualisieren Ihr Nachschlagewerk

- Get your subscription for the one and only newspaper for hobbyists

- Multi-coloured and full of the latest news and information on fishes and aquarium keeping

- Includes Stickups of the newest discoveries and breeding forms for keeping your AQUALOG book up-to-date

news;

Apistogramma sp. "PANDURINI"

S03775-3 Apistogramma sp. aff. payaminonis Sunset-Apistogramma Peru: middle course of the Rio Ucayali
Photo: U.Römer

r, Aquarianer !
porters, dealers, and hobbyists

books;

- Zeigen Ihnen immer alle Fische der jeweiligen Gruppe

- *Features all fishes of one group in a separate volume*

- 500 - 900 exzellente Farbfotos, auch aller Varianten und Zuchtformen

- *500 - 900 brilliant colour photographs, including all varieties and breeding forms*

- Codenummern und Pflegesymbole machen die Bestimmung einfach und weltweit unverwechselbar

- *Easy symbol-text for care instructions plus ingenious code-numbers for fish identification, used the world over*

- Mit einzigartigem Ergänzungssystem

- *Unique supplement system*

og

..... rund um Ihr Hobby !
... for professional identification !

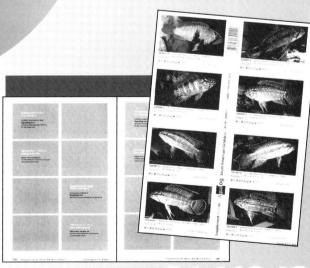

- Mit den regelmäßig erscheinenden Ergänzungsbögen garantieren wir Ihnen, daß Ihre Aqualog-Bildbände dauerhaft auf dem neuesten Stand sind.

- *The regularly published supplements guarantee a long-lasting, complete catalogue*

supplements;

Australia
Sydney Killie Group
c/o Parramatta Aquarium
PO Box 1117
Parramatta NSW 2150
Australia

Austria
DKG-Regionalgruppe Wien
Hans Gamperl
Marchfeldstraße 14/4/7/25
A-1200 Wien

Belgium
Association Killiphile Francophone de
Belgique (A.K.F.B.)
Jean Pol Vandersmissen
rue des Haies 77
B-6001 Marcinelle

Belgium
Belgische Killifish Vereniging
(B.K.V.)
Marcel Wuyts
Massenhovensesteenweg 2a
B-2520 Broechem-Ranst

Canada
Canadian Killifish Association (CKA)
Chris Sinclair
1251 Bray Court
Mississauga, Ontario L5J 3S4
Canada

Danmark
Skandinaviska Killi Sällskapet
(S.K.S.)
Peter Kirchhoff
Holte Stationsvej 16
DK-2840 Holte

France
Killi Club de France
(K.C.F.)
Daniel Poliak
9, rue Lusien Oriol
F- 77570 Chateau Landon

Germany
Deutsche Killifisch Gemeinschaft e.V.
(DKG)
Markus Thun
Oskar-Hoffmann-Straße 161
D-44789 Bochum

New Zealand
New Zealand Killifish Association (NZKA)
Kevin Rowe
39a Te Kupe Rd
Paraparaumu
New Zealand

Spain
Sociedad Española de Cyprinodóntidos
(SEC)
Dr. Franzisko Malumbres
El Algabeno 86
E-28043 Madrid

Sweden
Skandinaviska Killi Sällskapet
(S.K.S.)
Gunnar Åsblom
Mejerivägen 55
S 439 36 Onsala

Switzerland
DKG-Regionalgruppe Bodensee
Otto Binkert
St. Galler Straße 219
CH-9320 Stachen/Arbon

The Netherlands
Killi Fish Nederland
(K.F.N.)
Fred Kaijser
Bergstraat 13
NL 4641 RD Ossendrecht

United Kingdom
British Killifish Association
(B.K.A.)
Richard Cox
18, Nettleton Close, Poole
Dorset. BH17 8PL

U.S.A.
The American Killifish Association, Inc.
(A.K.A.)
903 Merrifield Place
Mishawaka, Indiana 46544

Anmerkung:
Sämtliche Angaben ohne Gewähr, Irrtum vorbehalten. Die Liste erhebt keinen Anspruch auf Vollständigkeit.

Please note:
All information without guarantee. This list may not be complete.

Key to the
Symbols   **fold out** ➞